AUTHORITY IN RELIGION

AUTHORITY IN RELIGION

BY

EDWARD GRUBB, M.A.

"As for you, the anointing which ye received of him abideth in you, and ye need not that any one teach you ; but as his anointing teacheth you concerning all things, and is true, and is no lie, even as it taught you, abide in him."—I *John ii.* 27.

NEW YORK

THE MACMILLAN COMPANY

1924

Printed in Great Britain by Fox, Jones & Co., Kemp Hall Press, Oxford.

PREFACE

THIS small book is based upon the author's *Authority and the Light Within*, published in 1908, which has gone through two editions and is now out of print. A considerable part of that book, devoted to a critical exposition of Quaker thought, has been omitted, but the author's main conception remains the same. Use has also been made of his pamphlet, *The Problem of Authority in Religion*, 1911. His thanks are due to the publishers of both for permission to use material therein contained, without the encumbrance of quotation marks. He wishes here to avow his indebtedness to many of the writings of the Dean of St. Paul's, Dr. W. R. Inge, from whom he has learnt much. Mention should also be made of Dr. Martineau's *Seat of Authority in Religion*, though its standpoint is somewhat different from that here adopted.

The book is not intended for theological experts. Its main purpose is to help young men and women, who are in perplexity because of the breakdown of the infallible outward authorities that have been supposed to control men's beliefs, and to encourage them to trust more fully to the inward authority with which Truth and Beauty and Goodness appeal to the normally constituted mind. If they will do this, the outward authorities will not be set aside, but each of them will find its fitting place. A full-rounded Christian faith cannot dispense with the legitimate authority of either Church or Bible, still less with that of Jesus Christ ; but none of these are of avail without the insight that comes of personal

v

and collective Christian experience. Nor can they be permitted to fetter free enquiry into truth by the methods of science and philosophy, of historical study, and of the criticism of the Bible and other religious writings which this involves. If such studies are undertaken in the spirit of reverent search for the Divine in nature and in manhood, they may correct, but do not negate, the intuitions of the Christian soul.

> " Still holy lives
> Reveal the Christ of whom the letter told,
> And the new gospel verifies the old."

EDWARD GRUBB.

LETCHWORTH.
February 1924.

CONTENTS

vii

His sayings—Sources of belief in His
Divine nature : this left assurance of His
real humanity unimpaired—The meaning
of " Kenosis " : in becoming truly man
He did not cease to be Divine—But He
was compassed with limitation : how far
this affects His authority.

Small use made by Apostles of words or
deeds of Jesus—His authority was that of
His living Spirit in their hearts : and
therefore inward—The Spirit a gift for the
Church at large and all its members : in
what sense " new "—Human personality
fulfilled in the life of the Spirit—The Spirit
in early Quaker thought : failure of attempt to make it an infallible " rule."—
Authority of the Spirit not outward.

Recognition of a Divine Light in man
does not render needless the saving work
of Christ—The inward eye partially blinded
by Sin—Need of reconciliation and enlightenment—The light of Christ in the
heart.

The necessary place of Authority : the
Church, the Bible, Jesus Christ, the Spirit
—The Spirit an adequate safeguard for
the Unity of the Church.

CHAPTER I

AUTHORITY, OUTWARD AND INWARD

WE are all aware that a great part of our lives is spent under Authority. In our earliest years, at home, we were subject to the authority of parents; when we were sent to school our doings were controlled by masters and mistresses. Throughout life we are under the authority of the Government, which in a democratic country represents the whole community, and which regulates our actions through laws administered by judges, magistrates, police, and a host of other officials. The individual is never an isolated unit; he grows up and maintains his life in relation, and largely in subjection, to the Society in which he finds himself; he is, all through life, compassed round with Authority. We do not start life without capital; we enter upon the accumulated inheritance of the ages. Even in the country that is most free, where thought is untrammelled by State or Church, our ideas and beliefs are in large part moulded by others. Few of us have ever had the opportunity of forming really independent conclusions, even on the theories that underlie the commonest concerns of life. For the most part we accept from others belief in the earth's rotation, in the chemical constitution of the air we breathe and the food we eat, in the outline of the history of our country, without having ourselves ever put these things to the test. All of us who are not original investigators, and many who are, in hundreds of matters, every day we live, accept the statements of other people whose knowledge and honesty we have no reason to doubt. Every person who can see further than others into the truth of things speaks with some authority, and that authority is generally recognised.

We have, of course, the power to set Authority at defiance : children disobey, men break the laws, new theories are started in opposition to those commonly accepted. Some people tell us we are living in an age of general revolt against Authority ; but this seems to be a perennial impression in the minds of the older generation, especially in times of rapid change and development such as that in which we live to-day. However this may be, it is certain that some defiance of the "dead hand" of traditional authority, even though accompanied with a measure of lawless self-assertion on the part of the individual, is one of the very conditions of progress. In primitive societies the beliefs and actions of men and women are for the most part ruled by authoritative custom ; they think and do, without questioning, what they suppose has always been thought and done. In such a society life becomes static and even stagnant ; there is no advance, and there may be grave degeneration. And, even in a society which is in the main progressive, foolish superstitions often show astonishing vitality. There are educated persons among us who would not walk under a ladder, or sit down thirteen at table, for fear of "bad luck." This can only mean that they accept at their face value statements that have been made to them, asking no questions and craving no evidence of their truth. It is defiance of such traditional authority that has won for us most of the liberties we now enjoy ; at the foundation of our science lies the revolt against authority made by men like Copernicus, Roger Bacon and Galileo.

It follows, therefore, that the authority over the individual which can rightfully be exercised by other people, or by the community as a whole, is not final or absolute, but is limited and relative. The attempt to make it more than this is self-destructive. For Society is composed of individuals ; and it is only as the individual expands, develops and grows strong that Society itself prospers. To crush the individual, as he was crushed under the mediæval Church, and as some think he would be crushed in a modern " collectivist " Utopia, is to destroy the very material out of which a vigorous society can be built up.

The Authority that seeks to direct and control the thoughts and actions of an individual from outside himself may be distinguished as Outward Authority. When the word Authority is used alone, it is generally the outward kind that is in view, and in what follows the endeavour will be made to use it with this meaning. But there is another kind. When we are driven to accept a statement, not because anyone else makes it, but because we see for ourselves that it is true, we may say that it exerts upon us an Inward Authority. Some may question whether this inward coercion should be called Authority at all. It seems advisable, for certain purposes, so to extend the meaning of the word, because there certainly is such a thing as inward compulsion to truth and also to goodness. " It moves, for all that," said Galileo, when he had been condemned for holding that it is the earth that moves and not the sun. Civilised humanity has

abandoned the attempt to coerce the beliefs of
individuals (unless in time of war), simply because it
has been found impossible to do it. " We needs must
love the highest when we see it," Tennyson truly wrote,
implying that the reason why we often do not love
it is that we do not really " see " it. The Inward
Authority that compels us by its own inherent force
to acceptance of what presents itself to us as True,
and Beautiful, and Good, is the Light Within of which
the Mystics speak.

The right development of Outward Authority is
a course of gradual self-suppression, in order that it
may give place to Inward Authority. The wise
parent endeavours to train his children to obey the
right from choice, not from compulsion ; the true
teacher draws his pupils on to form their own opinions
from independent examination of the facts. That
State is the healthiest in which the law is least often
put in motion, in which individuals have been so
taught and trained that they do of themselves such
things as the law directs. " Like every good teacher,"
says Auguste Sabatier, " Authority should labour to
render itself useless."[1] Good actions done under
compulsion are only half good ; true ideas accepted
at second hand are only half true. The only real
goodness is that which is the free choice of the individual ; the only really effectual truth is that which
he sees for himself to be grounded in fact and reason.
Outward Authority is therefore a means to an end,
not an end in itself.[2] Yet we must not go too fast
in trying to replace it with Inward Authority. We

[1] *Religions of Authority and the Religion of the Spirit*, p. xxvii.
[2] " Authority pleads as its justification that it is the necessary
condition for the complete carrying out of the principle of personality." (Höffding, *The Philosophy of Religion*, p. 279.)

are all, more or less, in the position of children; we
can none of us know very much, from our own direct
knowledge, about this complicated world.   Nor can
we see very far into the consequences of our conduct.
If we would live rightly, we must give weight to the
moral teachings that have come down to us through
the experience of the race, just as a boy at school has
to give in to learning Algebra and other things that
he " can't see the use of " at the time.   No " prigs "
are more trying than the young people who decline to
believe in " anything they cannot see."   There is
obvious danger of intellectual and moral anarchy
if everyone feels free to believe, or imagines he can
safely do, whatever is " right in his own eyes."   For
real progress we must use the achievements of those
who have gone before us; and this means that
Outward Authority must continue to have a place,
though it should be a diminishing one, in our lives.

So far we have been dealing with Authority mainly
as it concerns matters of ordinary life and knowledge.
We have now to consider whether the case is different
in those regions of highest moment which we call
distinctively spiritual or religious—remembering that
Religion is not a *department* of life, but a spirit in
which the whole should be lived.   It does, however,
differ from ordinary experience in that here we pass
" behind the veil " of time and sense, and seek to
live in a right relation with an unseen God.   The way
seems dim to those whose spiritual senses are not
acute, and the cry for authoritative guidance is often
insistent.   The craving is strong within us for an
infallible criterion of truth and right, for someone
to tell us with absolute authority both what we ought

to believe and how we ought to act. In our ignorance and weakness it seems vain to hope that we, by our own efforts, can attain to truth of knowledge or truth of conduct. " O God, my boat is so small, and Thy ocean is so vast ! " There are many who will admit to the full what has been said about the limited and provisional character of Authority in common life, who yet in the religious sphere demand something more final and conclusive. They want an Outward Authority that is absolute and infallible.

This enquiry proceeds on the assumption that the word " God " represents a great Reality—of all realities the deepest and most fundamental. It is also assumed that some knowledge of this underlying Reality is possible to men. If these assumptions are admitted, then it will follow that the ultimate source of such knowledge, the ultimate Authority, can be nowhere else than in God Himself, and that this Authority is final, absolute, and infallible. But how is it *mediated* to men ? The knowledge of God is widely different from our knowledge of facts. God is not one great phenomenon among other phenomena ; He never was nor will be perceptible by men's outward senses. " God is Spirit " ; " no man hath seen God at any time " ; " eye hath not seen, nor ear heard, nor hath entered into the understanding of man " the richness of the communion with Himself by which our lives are to be perfected. If He speaks to us, it is not with the audible voice of a person clothed in flesh and limited in space and time ; nor is it in words that can be heard by the multitude. The voice of God may indeed be heard by men, but individually and in secret ; and what He has to say is greater than any human words can fully express. Unless in some way His communication of truth could take outward form, it could not be applied, in the simple way that facts can, to afford a common test of truth. His Spirit can never be a " rule," either of faith or practice.   The Divine Authority is Inward Authority.

Hence men have felt the need of some outward expression of the Divine Authority—some visible institution, or form of words, in which it may be (so to say) embodied and made available for men to use as a rule of belief and practice.   They have supposed that God has met this need by embodying His Authority in an infallible Church, or an infallible Bible ; or by Himself taking human form and speaking words which would thenceforward provide an absolute Outward Authority as to what is and what is not the truth of God.   In the chapters that follow, it is proposed to enquire how far these supposed infallible outward authorities have made good their claim ; and, if the conclusion is that they have failed to do so, what alternative there is in which the Christian mind can find rest and peace.   Meanwhile— assuming that an inward knowledge of God is possible for men, while knowledge with the outward senses, even when aided by the intellect, is not—we should note that there is a large field, even in the spiritual sphere, in which that limited and relative authority which has been already spoken of may find a place. That which anyone can discern of God, in his own religious experience, gives him, so far, a measure of authority ; those who " see " further than others, the prophets and apostles of humanity, have more authority.   He who came from God, and lived ever near to the Father's heart, had it without measure. Truth that God has made known to individuals concerning Himself, however imperfectly understood by themselves and imparted to others, has been recorded in literature and embodied in institutions. The religious experience of those who have gone before us has produced, and given form to, these partial expressions of His mind and will ; and each one of us, who seeks God for himself, will naturally therefore " put himself to school within a larger experience than his own." If he declines to expect that he can be saved the trouble of the search for God, by having truth infallibly dealt out to him by Church or Bible, he will consider it equally presumptuous to imagine that it is to be miraculously revealed to him *de novo*. He will make humble use of the authorities around him, remembering that they are not absolute and final ; that their function is to train him in original powers of spiritual perception ; that Outward Authority is but a means through which an Inward Authority may become the guide of his life.

CHAPTER II

AUTHORITY AND REASON

THE principle of Authority, especially in Religion, has often been brought into sharp contrast with Reason, and it has been supposed that they are essentially opposed to one another. Lord Balfour, for example, in his book *The Foundations of Belief*, says : " Authority, as I have been using the term, is in all cases contrasted with Reason, and stands for that group of non-rational causes, moral, social and educational, which produces its results by psychic processes other than reasoning."[1] He traces most of the upbuilding factors in our life to Authority, and many of the destructive ones to Reason. " Reasoning," he says, " is a force most apt to divide and disintegrate." Similarly Mr. Benjamin Kidd, in *Social Evolution*, treated Reason as a selfish and short-sighted faculty which leads men to act always for what they think to be their own interests, and which needs to be continually held in check by the non-rational authority of Religion.

It may well be questioned whether anyone does service to Religion or its Authority by presenting it as irrational. There is, no doubt, some excuse for this view. Defenders of religious dogma have often written of Reason as if it were an enemy, as when

[1] *Foundations of Belief*, p. 219.

they denounced Tom Paine. Some of them regarded Reason as totally corrupted and incapacitated by the Fall of man. The authority of the Church was invoked to condemn the views of Galileo, which he had reached by the use of his reasoning powers. When a house-maid tries to draw up a fire by placing a poker vertically across the bars, because she has always been told that the device is effective,[1] we wish she would use her reasoning powers and think the matter out. But there is not, after all, any real conflict between Reason and the *right* use of Authority, whether Outward or Inward. It is perfectly rational to trust to authorities in matters where we have not, and perhaps cannot have, personal knowledge, provided we have no ground for supposing that they are deceiving us, and are ready to question them should the need arise. And, as regards the Inward Authority which truth and beauty and goodness exert upon us, we shall see presently that this is identical with the power of Reason in a large sense of that term.

For the difficulty arises mainly from the fact that the word Reason, like many more, is used with different meanings. It is quite arbitrary to allow it only the narrow significance assigned to it by writers like Lord Balfour and Mr. Kidd. In its largest sense, Reason is identical with Self-consciousness. It is the Mind, Thought, or Intelligence that broadly distinguishes man from the rest of the animals, which appear to have little if any self-consciousness, and to be actuated by instinct and impulse rather than by intelligent purpose. The function of Reason is to apprehend *Truth*—another term which may

---

[1] It has been suggested that this was originally an attempt to make the sign of the cross, and so charm the fire into burning.

be correctly used in a large sense as covering *all that wins assent* from the rightly exercised mind : whether in the cognitive region of experience, as truth of Fact, in the æsthetic, as the truly Beautiful and lovely, and in the ethical, as the truly Good and right.[1]   In this wide sense, of course, the term Reason covers our knowledge of God.

But the word is often confined to a narrower meaning—namely, that particular activity of the mind by which we reach truth *through inference* : as when we say, " It must be raining, for the roofs are wet."   The use of the conjunction " therefore " is a mark of this department of thought.   Just in so far as the word " Reason " stands for this process of deliberate " Reasoning " or argument, it is in a certain opposition to Authority, both outward and inward.   Whatever we can prove to be true, by valid reasoning, we do not accept on anyone's authority. Nor, although it has undoubtedly a compelling power over our beliefs, can it be considered as exerting upon us what we have called Inward Authority. For the distinctive mark of that kind of authority is that it is direct and immediate : we accept something as true or beautiful or good, because we ourselves perceive it to be so.   When truth is reached by Reasoning, whatever authority it has is not direct, but is mediated to us through the steps of the argu-

---

[1] The " Ultimate Values " of life are these three—the True, the Beautiful, and the Good.   The word " Reason " is here used in its largest sense, for the power by which we apprehend them all.   It is, of course, a sad and disturbing part of our experience that we may and do turn aside from Truth, preferring fancies to facts, the unlovely to the beautiful, the wrong course to the right.   We are prone to Error and to Sin.   But this is because we do not always submit ourselves to the Inward Authority of Truth, or follow the Reason that assents to it as good.

ment. The great advantage of this mediate or
reasoned knowledge is that it is *communicable* to
others. What we can prove by valid argument is
true, not for ourselves alone, but for *all* who are of
sound mind and can follow the steps of the argument.
Hence Reason, in this sense of the term, is our principal
means of spreading knowledge and widening the field
of ascertained truth.

But there are vast tracts of experience, and these
among the most important for the purposes of life,
which cannot be made objects of cogent inference
and demonstration. Strictly logical reasoning can
only be applied to conceptions that are precisely
defined—for which words have been found, or invented, which cover an exact area of meaning, no
more and no less. But such conceptions, though they
are of enormous service in helping us to reach and
communicate truth intellectually, are, as Bergson has
abundantly shown, *abstract* in their character. They
are, he says, like snapshots taken by a camera at a
moving field of real things, and cannot represent
their inner reality, which is constantly changing. In
the world of nature as it really is, classes of things
fade off into each other by infinite gradations : no
definition we can frame even of important terms like
" animal " or " plant " is really adequate to the
infinite complexity of what we find. Real knowledge,
if we can have it, is of particulars ; intellectual knowledge, reached by reasoning, is but a convenient
simplification of reality ; it is abstract and sym-
bolical.[1] That is to say, even cognitive or intellectual
truth is partial and inadequate ; it does not fully
represent reality. Still less can we reach by reasoning

[1] So Bertrand Russell, *Some Problems of Philosophy.*

the truth of the other great values, Beauty and
Goodness.   These can never be precisely defined ;
we know good and beautiful objects when we see them
(though our eyes may be only partially opened to
perceive what is *truly* good), but we cannot possibly
express in words wherein their goodness and their
beauty consist.   Consequently, the presence of these
values can never be proved by argument, it can only
be perceived.

The same holds with our knowledge of *persons*.
We say we know a friend through his looks, his words,
his acts.   Yes ; but after all these are only signs of
something that lies behind—his real character or
personality.   And how do we know what these signs
mean ?   The answer is that we only know it by something in ourselves.   We can interpret these signs
because we have some experience ourselves of what it
is to be genial, humble, loving or the reverse.   Apart
from that the signs would convey nothing to us.
Persons are known to us by the response of our whole
personality to theirs.   They may be in a position to
exercise outward authority over us ; but it is by an
inward light that we know them for what they are.

This is true also of our knowledge of God, and of our
relation to Him—of all that is included in " Divine
truth."   There is no separate organ or faculty for the
apprehension of this deepest kind of knowledge.   We
know God because we are essentially His sons ; and
because the sonship within us rises up to meet our
Father.[1]   Truth in these regions of experience is
reached by a kind of intuition, in which true conclusions are arrived at without going through the
painful steps of deliberate reasoning.   " Reason "

[1] *Lux Mundi* (tenth edition), pp. 15–19.

in the large sense of the term is at work ; but it acts
by a kind of instinctive or implicit reasoning, which
may or may not, later on, be justified by conscious
demonstration, and so enable us in some measure
to communicate our knowledge to others.

There are those who object to the attempt to make
religious truth a matter of intellectual demonstration.
Apart altogether from the protest of the dogmatists
who imagine that human Reason is totally corrupted
by the Fall, which appears to cut away the ground from
all real knowledge of God,[1] there are many who
rightly feel that there is in religious truth an infinite
element such as cannot be confined within the precise
and definite conceptions with which the reasoning
intellect can properly deal. There is to-day an
impatience, which is largely healthy, with all dog-
matics—a feeling that religious thoughts are spoiled
and vulgarised by being subjected to processes of
analysis and definition. We cannot set down in a
catalogue the beauties of a sunset or a poem ; why
should we think of defining and systematising the
" attributes of God," or the meaning of Christ's
person and work ? Why should we refuse to entertain
religious ideas until we can make them the objects of
rounded demonstration ?

This is true and important ; yet there are some
things that Reason can do, even in the limited sense
of reasoning and argument, which are of great service
to religion, which reinforce the inward authority
which it exerts upon our lives, and enable us to
communicate our beliefs to others. In the first place,
sound reasoning can remove some of the obstacles
that make people reject all knowledge of God as an

[1] See below, p. 21, note.

attainment impossible for man. Here Philosophy can help in laying a basis for Faith. While at the present time there are divergent philosophies, there is increasing agreement that the old Materialism, which made Thought or Mind a mere product of matter and force, is quite out of court. Thought is understood to be the *prius* of all our knowledge of matter and force. Nothing is known at all except as related to Consciousness. The Mind that perceives relations among objects can be no mere product of the things related, nor can a stream of sensations organize experience into a unity.[1] We have experience ; our experience is not in detached or unrelated fragments, but forms itself into a cosmos or unity ; and this can only mean that what lies at the root of it is not matter but Mind or Reason. Many would go further than this and agree that the unity of *human*, as distinct from *individual*, experience, implies a Universal Mind or Consciousness, of which that of the individual is but (as it were) a focus-point or partial manifestation. If there were only individual minds, there might be as many truths as there are persons. The fact that we recognise only *one truth*, and all the rest as error, points to One Consciousness as that for which the whole world exists. God is seen to be the deepest foundation of all truth, the reality of which phenomena are but appearances, the basis of the distinction we make between truth and falsehood. The world is real, but it has its reality in God, and in God alone.[2] Human consciousness, or human personality, is thus regarded as a point at which the Universal Consciousness, or Divine Personality, is

[1] T. H. Green, *Prolegomena to Ethics*, passim.
[2] Rufus M. Jones, *Social Law in the Spiritual World*, pp. 238–245.

seeking to manifest itself. In Biblical language, man is made in the image of God. Reason, therefore, which in the widest sense is identical with Thought or Self-consciousness, is in a real sense not only human but Divine. In Johannine language, the Divine Logos or Reason was from the beginning with God and was God, and was also the Light of man. This is an example of the use of Reasoning to clear away obstacles from the path of faith in God.

In the second place, Reason may be just as usefully employed in ordering the material of religious knowledge as in constructing theories in other departments of study. It is obvious that the theory of sound will never make a musician, yet a musician may be the better for a knowledge of the theory. " Religion exists and must exist as a life and experience, before it can be made the object of reflective thought ; but there is no more reason in this than in other instances, why experimental knowledge should exclude scientific knowledge."[1] Such reasoned and " scientific knowledge " is what constitutes a sound Theology.

Thirdly, there is much for Reason to do in purifying the affirmations made on the basis of Authority, whether outward or inward, from the false elements that too easily enter into them. The errors of religious faith, the credulity into which it readily slips, need continual criticism by reason and argument. It is very easy, for example, to confuse the conventional framework of ideas, within which faith is accustomed to move about, with the inner kernel that is really its object, and to attribute the same reality to the one as to the other. A Roman Catholic

[1] John Caird, *Fundamental Ideas of Christianity*, Vol. I, p. 42. The whole of this chapter, " Faith and Reason," may well be read.

may have the same inward assurance of the help of the Virgin or the Saints that he has of Divine answer to his prayer. Yet a Protestant would feel sure that, while the latter is of the kernel, the former is merely of the framework. Such a separation of false elements from true is needed right through the range of Christian beliefs, and is only to be accomplished by the diligent use of enlightened Reason.

The upshot of this chapter, on a subject that is somewhat obscure and difficult, is that there is no necessary conflict between Authority and Reason. Both have their rightful places in constructing the fabric of our knowledge and ordering our beliefs. In the widest sense of the term, Reason is the guide to Truth—not only to intellectual knowledge, but to appreciation of the supreme Values that find their ultimate meaning and reality in God. And, in the more restricted sense of Reasoning, while this cannot yield cogent demonstration of the highest Reality, it is yet of great service in removing obstacles to Faith, building up our religious knowledge into a coherent whole, criticising the dependence on outward Authority that often degenerates into Credulity, and enabling us in some measure to communicate to others the truth whose inward Authority commands our souls.

CHAPTER III

THE AUTHORITY OF CONSCIENCE

THE region of experience in which Inward Authority is clearest is that of our moral life, which is, or ought to be, ruled by Conscience. Conscience has often been called " the voice of God within us," and its supreme authority has been powerfully set forth by Kant, Bishop Butler, and many other thinkers. Yet difficulties in regard to this are very widely felt. How is it that, if Conscience is the voice of God, it seems to say one thing to one man and another to another ? Why does a Moslem consider polygamy to be right and the drinking of alcohol wrong, while Christians are convinced that polygamy is wrong and many believe that the moderate consumption of alcohol is right ? Why have the judgments of people differed so widely in regard to the ethics of slavery, war, gambling, competition ?—to take only a few examples. These very varying judgments seem to discredit Conscience as an authoritative guide for life, or at any rate to weaken its authority. In a great national emergency we have seen men of unquestioned honesty of purpose and nobility of character, after severe inward struggle, reaching opposite conclusions as to what course of action their duty to God and man required : one choosing the hard path of offering his life for the defence of his country, and another the equally hard path of enduring the taunt of cowardice, and even severe punishment, by refusing, because he felt it would be wrong, to take any part in the slaughter of his fellowmen.

Many attempts have been made to " explain " the nature and origin of Conscience as the result of education—the effect upon the individual of his social environment, and the penalties it is able to inflict. Evolutionists like Herbert Spencer have tried to show that Conscience is the deposit left in the human race by its age-long struggle for existence ; it directs us to the conduct which centuries of experience have proved to possess survival value. In other words, that which we think to be right is what our ancestors found would pay in the long run. Now, while we may admit that right conduct " pays in the long run," it is not at all clear that the peculiar quality of Conscience can be explained by any considerations of prudence, even in the experience of the race. That quality is expressed in the small word " ought," which carries a conviction that is simply not contained in considerations of what will pay, or even in the fear of punishment. We have to face the fact that some people of great worth to society will endure any punishment rather than do what they believe to be wrong.

" It does not seem possible for any extension of our scientific knowledge to reduce conscience to a naturalistic explanation. Its power over us cannot be explained on the ground that it aids survival. The distinction of right and wrong does not rest, in the ultimate analysis, upon prudence, foresight, or any consideration of utilitarian results, in fact upon any extraneous or self-advantageous considerations. It cannot be reduced to a fine calculation of results. It cannot be traced to an emotion, or to an instinct, which aided survival, or to a racial habit or custom. We do not catch the secret of conscience by any study of the slow results of restraint or the fear of punishment, here or hereafter. The difficulty about the whole situation is that fear of consequences is not morality—it is fear of consequences." [1]

It would seem that Conscience is " the voice of God " within us in the same way that Reason is—for this, as was said in the last chapter, is in its largest sense not only human but Divine. Conscience is, in fact, the Reason that in the ethical sphere of experience distinguishes the true from the false.[2] The peculiarity of it is that in this region, where the will is primarily concerned, there is a unique consciousness of *obligation* to follow one course and reject another. Conscience is felt *to command the will* in a way that is not experienced in regard to matters of intellectual truth, or of æsthetic taste. In all cases of ultimate values Reason distinguishes the higher from the lower, and its inward authority compels us to accept the one and reject the other. But only in the ethical sphere, where the will is the primary agency at work, is there the sense of an inward *command*, and of condemnation if we choose amiss. This appears to be the reason why Conscience has been regarded as the voice of God, while the same

[1] Rufus M. Jones, *The Nature and Authority of Conscience*, pp. 44, 45.

[2] Compare 2 Cor. iv. 2 : " By manifestation of *the truth* commending ourselves to every man's *conscience* in the sight of God."

lofty quality has not been attributed to our intellectual and æsthetic judgments.[1]

If, then, we ask why Conscience appears to give varying deliverances, the answer would seem to be : for the same reason that we make mistakes in regard to the other values of life. Our Reason is imperfectly developed, and mistakes false statements for true ones, attributes beauty to objects that are not really lovely, and fancies actions are good and right when they are not. For long ages people believed the world to be a flat expanse, and the sky a material dome above it. Children (in years or mind) love brilliant colours, and are often insensitive to their discords ; they may prefer the chalk drawings on the pavement made by a wounded soldier to the Turner pictures in the National Gallery. In all cases there is *a true standard*—of accordance with fact, of real beauty, and of true goodness—though our Reason, at any given point of man's history, may be untrained

---

[1] A word should be said here concerning the nature of Sin. Sin differs from Error in that it is a voluntary choosing of that which is known to be the lower alternative. Strictly speaking, it is not sin to be mistaken as to a matter of fact, or to think that rose-pink and orange make a good combination of colours, or to believe that Slavery is right. Sin comes in when *the will* is at work : when we wilfully choose what we know to be a lower course, and reject what we know to be a higher. It is defiance of the Inward Authority; in the full sense of the term it is always " against the light." But (as we shall see later) it is characteristic of Sin that it impairs the inward eye and distorts the judgment—not only in moral questions, but in regard to Truth as a whole. Hence we cannot always say that those who fall into error are free from sin : in some cases they might, and ought to, have known better. We must also recognise that, while Sin cannot be inherited, it is extremely probable that *tendencies* to Sin can : that sin tends to a *racial* weakening of will and moral deterioration. This appears to be the truth of the old dogma of Original Sin. But the dogmatists who insisted that man is " totally corrupt " said what is obviously neither true to fact nor in accord with the plain teaching of Jesus Christ. Were it true that man possesses no inward power of response to goodnesss, the foundation could not be laid for either ethics or religion.

C

to appreciate it rightly. What is needed is the education and enlightenment of our Reason—and, most important of all, in that department of it which we call the Conscience. If a person (as might be possible) sincerely felt it to be his duty to kill his own children, to save them from the evil of this world, we should agree that his conscience badly needed enlightening.

Happily for man, his Conscience is capable of this education and enlightenment, and such illumination is the main secret of the progress of the race. It is because there is a Divine element in man that the illumination is possible. It is this, the spark of the Universal Reason, which makes him a self-determining agent, not a mere creature of impulse. It enables him to hold before his mind different ideals, and different courses of action tending to their realisation ; to picture himself as finding satisfaction in the achievement of one or another, and to decide which shall be the one with which he chooses to identify himself. It forces upon him the conviction that these ideals are often of different worth, as higher or lower ; and that, whatever the consequences may be, he " ought " to choose that which appears to him the higher.

It is the Divine Light in man that has gradually enlightened his Conscience, along with his intellect and his power of æsthetic appreciation, and has enabled him to rise from barbarism to comparative civilisation. From the first rude beginnings of human society, it was this that made man conscious, however dimly, that his life was bound up with the lives of others, that his inclinations must be curbed for the common good, that he " ought " not to transgress the limits set by authoritative custom.

We see it powerfully at work in the great ethical teachers of mankind, as in Socrates and the piercing questions with which he made his fellow-citizens aware of the poverty of their moral ideas. We see it best in the people of Israel—the race that beyond all others was sensitive on the ethical side, and was distinguished by a genius for morality. No study is more fascinating than that of the development of the Hebrew conscience. Starting, it appears, with ideas about God and His requirements but little removed from those of other Semitic tribes, we see prophet souls awakened to the conviction that it was not human sacrifice, nor even the slaughter of animals, that would satisfy God's requirements ; that the only sacrifice really pleasing to Him was that of man's inward heart and life for the doing of His will.[1] This new truth, which not only was not derived from current religious teaching, but ran entirely counter to the existing ideas of what constituted religion and bound a people to its God, brought upon the prophets fierce persecution ; but they did not cease to utter it. And, in time, the persecutors themselves, or their descendants, became convinced that it was true ; a new conscience was developed in the Hebrew mind, by the faithfulness to conviction of those who had first discerned the higher truth. It is hard indeed to account either for the perception of it by prophets and psalmists, or for its power to convince those who had at first opposed it, if there was not a Light from God in the souls of men, enlightening and educating their conscience.

[1] See especially Micah vi. 6–8, which is typical of the utterances of the greater prophets and psalmists : " What doth the Lord require of thee but to do justly, and to love mercy, and to walk humbly with thy God ? "

But the greatest of all examples of fidelity to Conscience is found in the career of Jesus Himself. Assured, at least from the time of the experience that followed His baptism, that it was His task to bring to men the Kingdom of God, yet equally convinced that both the Kingdom and its Messiah were not to be of the kind that His people were expecting ; seeing clearly that to forgo the outward displays of power that they were looking for would mean His probable rejection and death as a pretender to Messiahship ; He yet kept steadily before His eyes the work which He believed His Father had given Him to do, and trod, almost in solitude, the pathway to the Cross.

" The word conscience is never used in the gospels, but that inner tribunal which we name by that word is nowhere more clearly in evidence than in the stages of the decision that carried Jesus to the cross, in dedication to the untried but ultimately irresistible power of redeeming love. He emphasizes at every point the nearness of the divine to the human in man, the infinite preciousness of the individual soul, the dramatic issues of the inner life, the fateful decisiveness of moral choices, the fact that the Kingdom of God is an interior spirit and not an external power. It is just because these truths are true that conscience can be the mighty force which it is." [1]

The greatest achievement of Jesus Christ, regarding Him for the moment merely as an ethical Leader, was to awaken men to the consciousness of human Brotherhood—the Unity of the race of men. To Greek and Jew alike, the idea of universal Brotherhood, if it had occurred at all, seemed mere fanatical folly. The Greek felt the tie of common duty to

[1] R. M. Jones, *The Nature and Authority of Conscience*, pp. 21, 22.

fellow-Greeks, but hardly, if at all, to barbarians, slaves, or women. The Jew thought himself right in hating Samaritans and Gentiles. It is true that a few Roman Stoics and jurists had discerned, even before Christ came, that mankind is bound together by ties that go deeper than race or nation;[1] but this remained a poetic sentiment in the minds of a very few, and appears to have had no influence on the conduct of the mass of men. It was Jesus who first made it " current coin." By His teaching and practice He definitely widened the area of " neighbour "-hood to cover all mankind ; and placed it, for those who accepted Him, on the firm basis of a Divine revelation, making it a necessary consequence of the universal Fatherhood of God.

But this idea of Brotherhood, like that of spiritual sacrifice which dawned on the minds of the greater prophets and psalmists, was contrary to the ingrained beliefs of the time. It struck directly some of the most venerable institutions of the ancient world, like the Gladiatorial games and Slavery ; and of the mediæval world, like Feudalism ; and in the end it shattered them. How was this possible ? Only because there was something of God in men which enabled them to discern its truth ; which forced them to the conviction that, being higher than their old ideals, it must be followed ; which gradually formed in them a new and more enlightened Conscience.

The process of enlightenment, in which Christianity is the leading factor, is very far as yet from being completed. The civilised nations have, indeed (in theory at least), put an end to Slavery, and to the

---

[1] For examples see Lecky, *History of European Morals*, Vol. I, pp. 240, 241.

exploitation of women for the convenience of men. But war still has " Christian " defenders, and during the late conflict the hatred of Germans was proclaimed from high quarters as a duty to our own people. The statesmanship of great nations is still based avowedly on undiluted national selfishness. It is widely held that the desire for gain is the right and proper motive in business. And few are yet sensitive to the injustice which denies, to the great masses of our people, who do for us the hard manual work of life, any share in that heritage of culture and refined enjoyment without which, to us who have it, life would be almost worthless.

For the further enlightenment of the social conscience of mankind we must trust to the same Divine Light which has developed it hitherto. If we have this confidence, we can regard with calmness the adjustments of the social, industrial and international fabric of human society which are necessary if the Christian ideal of Brotherhood is to be realised. If the underlying aim of these adjustments is presented as the liberation of the human spirit from the shackles that now restrain its development, and not the mere redistribution of material goods, then there need be no " class war." For more and more the possessors of wealth will be found, as many of them have been and are at present, on the side of the dispossessed— because their conscience is enlightened enough to perceive that the aim is a good one, and that they ought to promote it. The inevitable conflict will be peaceful and fraught with permanent results ; it will be a conflict, not of classes with one another, but between those in all classes whose conscience is enlightened and those in whom it is not.

The hardest problems that Conscience presents to us come when Duties seem to conflict with one another —especially when duty to our own nation appears opposed to our duty to humanity at large. To many ardent young men the Conscription Acts brought such a problem. What were they to do, when duty to God or humanity seemed to lead one way, and duty to their country in another? The only course, in such a conflict, is surely to weigh, prayerfully, and with all the light that reason and history and Christian principles can supply, the relative moral worth of the two courses; and, having decided which appears to be as the higher, to follow it at all costs. Though others, equally conscientious, might decide the matter differently, for the individual there is no real clash of duties; in following that which appeals to him as the higher, he is really discharging the other to the best of his ability.

> " I could not love thee, dear, so much
>   Loved I not honour more "

said the Elizabethan lover, called to leave the side of his mistress for what he believed to be a larger duty. If it is true that many of the men who chose war service thought they were joining in a great struggle for human liberty, it is equally true that many who refused it were sure that by their faithfulness to conviction they were rendering a higher service, even to their own country, than if they had fought on its behalf.

The Conscription Acts revealed an extraordinary lack of understanding of the claims of Conscience on the part of many who might have been supposed to know better. Members of the Tribunals, which were set up to examine the reality of a man's conscientious objection to war, openly stated that they believed it to be " humbug." [1] The whole episode was depressing and humiliating, but it showed very clearly the impossibility of any human authority deciding with accuracy and justice the state of other men's consciences. It may well be questioned whether it is ever within the province of a rightly-ordered State to coerce its members in matters of life and death— even in the case of so-called " political objectors," who, not convinced that War under all conceivable circumstances is wrong, yet demand that their consciences shall be free to decide whether a particular war is just or unjust, and that they shall not be compelled to aid in the taking of human life for a cause they believe to be wrong.

So much it seems right to say on some of the difficulties presented by Conscience when its inward authority comes into conflict with the outward authority wielded by the State. It seems very clear that there is abundant need for the further enlightenment, by the Spirit of God, of the consciences of us all, whether professing Christians or not. Jesus Christ, we may be thankful, made no attempt to construct a new Decalogue, crystallising in a formula the moral duties of men. He left the field open for indefinite expansion, and trusted His own living Spirit to afford the necessary enlightenment from age to age. He contented Himself with two commandments—love to God and love to men—which are not so much precepts as an expression of the ultimate moral basis : that life must be lived in a right relation

---

[1] See Graham, *Conscription and Conscience*, pp. 68–97. Also pp. 42–45.

to our spiritual environment, both in the unseen and the seen. It is on this basis that every ethical system, in every age, must always rest.[1]

It has been shown that the variation, from age to age, and from one social group to another, of the moral standard by which men live, is no disproof of the reality of a Divine Light within their souls. The moral standard *must* vary, according to the degree of ethical enlightenment men have reached. No single " duty," nor the nature of the moral good which informs all " duties," is so completely known to us that it can be adequately and finally expressed in any form of words. There is in it something of the infinite—something of the nature of God Himself—so that our knowledge of it is ever growing, never complete.[2] No empirical moral judgment is ever final or exhaustive ; and this fact may comfort us in some of our moral perplexities.[3]

Yet we are not thereby in any degree absolved from the necessity of seeking ever for the highest ; nor deprived of the happy faith that each surrendered will and obedient heart may know, if the inward eye is ever open to the Light, the priceless blessing of " a conscience void of offence."

[1] See *Ecce Homo*, chapter on " The Enthusiasm of Humanity."

[2] See T. H. Green, *Prolegomena to Ethics*, pp. 178 *ff*.

[3] The fact, for example, that it is no easy matter so to define War as to say precisely what use of force constitutes War, is no reason for doubting the dictum of the enlightened Christian conscience, that War is wrong.

CHAPTER IV

AUTHORITY AND FAITH

WE come now to the heart of our subject, for we have to consider the right relation between Authority and the Faith that is the vital organ of the religious life. We cannot reach a conclusion without some enquiry as to the nature of Faith. It has been very widely held that Faith is essentially uncritical submission to an outward Authority, in matters that are beyond the reach of Reason. " I should not believe the Gospel," said Augustine, " unless the authority of the Catholic Church moved me to do so."[1] This is the orthodox Roman Catholic view of Faith, and the " simple faith " enjoined on us by some Evangelical Protestants is of exactly the same kind. We are to believe in Christianity, and in special " doctrines " not because we ourselves perceive them to be true, but because they are taught in the Bible, and the Bible is " the Word of God." Faith is thought of as the blind acceptance of " information imparted by a higher Power, which must be accepted uncritically because, *ex hypothesi*, we are incapable of criticising it." That is what, in the strictest sense, Authority in Religion means,[2] and Faith is supposed to be its correlative.

[1] *Contra Ep. Manich.*, 6, quoted in *Dictionary of Religion and Ethics*, article " Faith," Vol. V, p. 690.

[2] Inge, *Authority and the Inner Light*, Liverpool Diocesan Lecture, 1912.

In later chapters we shall have to examine carefully the claims of the outward Authorities to which men have submitted themselves.

Meanwhile it may be pointed out that this idea of Faith as submission to Authority began very early in the history of the Church. Irenæus and Tertullian, towards the close of the second century, declared to be " heretical " whatever was not contained in the " rule of faith " supposed to have been handed down by the Apostles. In the latest books of the New Testament, as in the Pastoral Epistles and that attributed to Jude, " the faith " has already come to be regarded as a deposit of apostolic teaching which is to be taken without question : " contending earnestly," says Jude, in a passage dear to the heart of Biblical authoritarians, " for the faith once for all delivered to the saints." [1]

But this idea of Faith as a passive and almost blind submission to, and acceptance of, an Authority believed to be Divinely certified, is far indeed from being the prevailing Biblical conception. In the Old Testament the word is scarcely ever used : though the writers were full of the experience, they had not yet found the word by which to express it. In the only two places where it occurs,[2] it probably has a similar meaning to that which the corresponding words πίστις and *fides* bear in Greek and Latin : that is, *faithfulness* or the keeping of promises, as when we say a person acts " in good faith." In all these languages the meaning was easily extended to cover the *mutual confidence* of those who have entered into

[1] Jude, *v.* 3.
[2] Deut. xxxii. 20, " Children in whom is no faith " ; and Hab. ii. 4, " The just shall live by his faith."—(R.V. margin, " in his faithfulness.")

an agreement, that the other party is going to keep
it ; hence the Hebrew word could have been, though
apparently it was not, used to express the *trust* in
God, the assurance that He would keep His covenant
with His people, which marked the lives of the Old
Testament saints. In the Gospels and Acts it
sometimes has this meaning, as in Mark xi. 22,
" Have faith in God " ; but more often it is used to
express confident expectation of receiving help from
Jesus, or from God through Him.[1] Specially instruc-
tive is the " faith " of the Roman centurion mentioned
in Matt. viii. 5–10, which Jesus commended as "greater
than any in Israel." Just as he felt he had the whole
power of the Roman Empire behind him, as long as
he was loyal and obedient, so he was sure that Jesus
had behind Him the limitless resources of God.
The word comes to mean *insight* into the character
and worth of Jesus, and assurance of His power to
help and save.

From this it is an easy transition to the specialised
meaning which the word " faith " mostly has in the
epistles of Paul—belief in, and acceptance of, the
saving grace manifested in Jesus Christ. While he
brings the faith by which we are " justified " into
contrast with " works of righteousness," it is clear
that he regards it as a *condition* of good works, not as a
substitute for them : the first thing for living the
righteous life is that we should be set right with God
by making our own the forgiveness, and the reconciliation with Himself, which He offers us in Christ.
If we seek for righteousness in this way, as contrasted
with the Pharisaic method, we shall never suppose
that we have *earned* salvation by any merit of our

[1] *E.g.* Mark ii. 5, Matt. ix. 27–30, Luke vii. 50, Acts xiv. 9, etc.

own. Faith is acceptance of God's gift in Christ and
acting upon it.

The author of the Epistle to the Hebrews uses the
word in a much more general sense, as " the substance
(or assurance) of things hoped for, the proving of
things not seen " (Heb. xi. 1). It is the power by
which we live in touch with the unseen world—the
world of *realities* of which material things are but
shadows. Paul also sometimes uses the word in a
similar large sense, as when he says " we walk by
faith, not by sight " (2 Cor. v. 7). This contrast
with " sight " is frequent in the New Testament, but
not once is opposition suggested between faith and
reason, and never is the word " faith " used for a
blind acceptance of truth upon authority. Nor does
it mean a merely intellectual acceptance of statements
about God or Christ ;[1] rather it is an insight by which
we pierce for ourselves into the Reality that lies
hidden below the surface of the world of ordinary
experience, and an energy of the soul by which we act
in accordance with what we find there. " The
truth " is that which commends itself to a man's
" conscience " (2 Cor. iv. 2). An essential part of
the prodigal's faith in his father was that " he arose
and came."

Faith, then, is in the New Testament not a blind
submission to an outward authority, but rather a

---

[1] Such a meaning has been supposed to underlie some passages
in the fourth Gospel and the first Epistle by the same writer (see
E. F. Scott, *The Fourth Gospel*, p. 119, etc.) ; but this seems un-
warranted. The writer avoids abstract terms and hardly ever uses
the word " faith." But his " believing," as Mr. Scott says elsewhere (p. 269) is " assent to the claim of a person," and as such is
much deeper than an assent to facts. It involves the will, just as
" truth " for this writer is something that has to be " done " (John
iii. 21).

keen-eyed response to the *inward* authority with
which God speaks to man through Nature, through
Conscience, through History, and most of all through
Jesus Christ. What happened in the second century
was really a *loss* of faith. It was because men had no
longer the first insight into truth, that they felt the
need of a " rule of faith " to prevent them from losing
truth altogether. It was when the light that Christ
had kindled within them was burning dim, that they
sought about for an infallible outward guide. And
the setting up of such a " rule " could give a respect-
able account of itself. Faith had always meant trust
in God ; and if He had embodied His authority in a
" rule of faith," any apparent departure from it, or
doubt cast upon its infallible accuracy, seemed like a
doubt of God Himself. Trust in God was interpreted
as compelling a literal acceptance of all He was
supposed to have revealed, even if some of this
appeared impossible or absurd. " It is credible,"
wrote Tertullian in an intentional paradox, of the
death and resurrection of Jesus, " because it is foolish ;
it is certain because it is impossible."[1] The words
have often been used in ways he did not intend ;
but they express in an extreme form the attempt to
place Faith on a basis of outward Authority in
defiance of Reason. It should be noted that when we
accept a truth upon authority, our belief is really not
in the truth itself but in the authority on which it is
supposed to rest.

It is, as has been said above,[2] perfectly legitimate

[1] Glover, *Conflict of Religions in the early Roman Empire*, p. 341.
Also Inge, *Faith and its Psychology*, p. 30. The whole of the latter
book is full of instruction ; especially (for our present subject)
chapters V, VI and VII, " Authority as a Ground of Faith."
[2] Chapter II, p. 10.

and reasonable to believe statements on Authority, *provided the authority is trustworthy*. But how are we to be convinced of this ? The question has not been sufficently considered. An Authority cannot prove itself trustworthy by mere assertion of its own infallibility ; you cannot prove Scripture infallible by quoting the text of the Authorised Version, " All Scripture is given by inspiration of God."[1] If this were possible, we should certainly have to accept the Koran as the direct " Word of God " ; for no sacred book makes higher claims for itself. " By the star when it setteth, your companion Muhammad erreth not, nor is led astray, neither doth he speak of his own will. It is none other than a revelation which hath been revealed to him."[2] Nor can the worth of an authority be proved by any external argument, as that he who claims to be speaking in God's name can work miracles. The inference is worthless ; it was rejected by our Lord Himself when He refused a sign from heaven (Mark viii. 11, 12) ; and, even if it had any force, belief in the miracles, if we have not witnessed them ourselves, usually rests on the very authority they are supposed to certify. It is absurd to try to support the authority of the Bible by miracles which we only believe in because they are in the Bible.

The real answer to the puzzle is that Outward Authority can only prove itself trustworthy by its own Inward Authority. We accept it because it appeals to a witness within ourselves that it is worthy of acceptance. The prophet can only " com-

[1] 2 Tim. iii. 16. The Revised Version has " Every Scripture inspired of God is also profitable for teaching, etc."

[2] Koran, liii. 1. Quoted in *Encycl. of Rel. and Eth.*, art. " Inspiration (Muslim)," Vol. VII, p. 354.

mend his message to us by awaking a response in our own hearts."

" This is in reality the only way in which a revelation is or can be made to us. The revelation comes to us with authority from outside, as the voice of God. The true prophet at any rate sincerely believes that God is speaking through his mouth ; and those who hear him are constrained to believe it too. Our hearts leap out to meet his words ; we recognise that this is what we wanted ; that here is the truth which we could not find for ourselves, the good news which we should not have dared to believe. We recognise in the prophet himself a man of God. We trust him instinctively ; when he speaks to us about the unseen world, we feel that he knows what he is speaking about, that he ' has been there ' himself. When we read the words of Jesus Himself, our hearts tell us that even this language is inadequate.

" This will show why I regard prophetical authority as a second ground of Faith. It is not independent of the primary ground, the inward tribunal which accepts or rejects it. It is this primary ground which alone makes belief on authority a religious act. Without it, belief in authority is inert opinion, or lazy acquiescence, or blind partisanship ; and none of these things has anything to do with Faith." [1]

Real Faith, then, is submission not to outward but

[1] Inge, *Faith and its Psychology*, pp. 81, 82. Jeremiah appealed, not in vain, to a witness within the hearts of his people that what he said to them was really from God (Jer. xxvi. 10–16). At a later time he tried to set up as a test between himself and the " false prophets " the external argument of the fulfilment of what had been foretold (xxviii. 9). But this led him into dire straits when apparently it gave the advantage to his opponents (xxxvii. 5–15), and in any case it was not a test that could be immediately applied.

to inward Authority—the authority of Truth itself, when this is concerned with unseen things—with God and our relation to Him. In some cases, indeed, it may be *aroused* within us by outward authority, especially when this is exerted by a person of intense character and deep spiritual life. As Tennyson writes of Galahad and Percival's sister :

" She sent the deathless passion in her eyes
  Through him, and made him hers, and laid her mind
  On him, and he believed in her belief." [1]

But the vision only came to Galahad when his faith had become his own and not another's. The author of the Fourth Gospel illustrates the progress from second-hand to real faith when he represents the Samaritans as saying, " Now we believe, not because of thy speaking ; for we have heard for ourselves, and know that this is indeed the Saviour of the world " (John iv. 42). And all the Mystics, from Paul and " John " onwards, have always insisted that real Faith is personal insight into the Truth of God. Thus Weigel, a Lutheran mystic, wrote :

" Knowledge must well out from within, and must not be introduced merely by a book, for this is in vain. It is the most mischievous deception when that which is most important is rejected. We put out a person's own eye, and then try to persuade him that he ought to see with someone else's eye." [2]

There is no conflict between Faith and Reason (in the large sense of the latter term) ; the real contrast is (as the New Testament says) between Faith and

---

[1] In *The Holy Grail.*
[2] Quoted by Inge, *op. cit.*, p. 115.

D

" Sight " ; and the latter term must be taken to cover truths that we perceive by the outward senses or prove by intellectual demonstration. " Seeing is believing," but it is not faith. Strict proof, ocular or logical, leaves no field for faith to work in. Faith, in its very nature, involves a leap *beyond* that which has been seen or proved, a *venture* of the whole man, feeling will and thought, into a world not yet fully explored. So do all human relations when they are at their best. We trust the persons we love far beyond what we have proved, and usually our trust is justified and our experience widened as otherwise it could not have been. Especially, Faith is like the venture of an ideal marriage, where each takes the other " for better or worse," facing with a joyous heart all that the unknown future may bring. Such faith " usually " verifies itself in experience ; but true faith in God *always* brings its own reward. Just as a time comes when each young swallow has to venture from the nest and cast itself upon the invisible air, so we have to let ourselves go upon that which we cannot see or prove to ourselves in any other way. The venture will succeed, for " underneath are the everlasting Arms." As Mr. Clutton-Brock put it :

" No man has a right to more faith than he has earned ; and the only way to earn faith is to act upon it before it comes." [1]

" Faith is not merely a function of thought, but a basal energy of the whole man. It includes an element of will ; and the office of will is not to register experience, but to make it." [2]

We conclude, then, that Faith is a native endowment

[1] *More Thoughts on the War*, p. 82 (slightly altered).
[2] Inge, *op. cit.*, p. 53.

of the human person as essentially the child of God. It is the sonship within us arising to meet the Father of our spirits.   Like all native endowments, which are gifts of God, it grows with exercise, and this requires the venture by which we project our grasp of Truth beyond that which is fully proved.   Its seat lies deeper in the self than the superficial distinctions we make between Emotion, Thought, and Will ; and in its exercise all these functions are involved.   Reason and Conscience are its friends and supporters, if they are also at times its necessary critics.   It may be kindled into activity by outward Authority, but it is never bound and fettered by any bonds that Authority can lay upon it.   It is the free response of the human soul to the inward Authority which assures us that truth and goodness and beauty speak to us with the very voice of God.

CHAPTER V

THE AUTHORITY OF THE CHURCH

THE craving for an infallible outward authority in religion arises from the nature of spiritual or religious truth. The deepest truth, the centre of our life and thought, the basis of all reality, is not to be discovered by our outward senses or proved by the logical reason. God is deeper than all phenomena, and He cannot, like matters of ordinary knowledge, be subjected to sensuous or intellectual demonstration. We cannot appeal to facts and say " Lo here ! " or " Lo there ! " We walk by faith, not by sight ; eye hath not seen, nor ear heard, nor the understanding of man conceived, the things of the Spirit. God manifests Himself to the inner consciousness ; His witness is within.

It is because men are afraid to trust this inward witness that they set about to find and establish an outward authority by which the declarations of the inward witness may be tested and controlled. They want some Divine institution, some external " rule " of faith and life, which may be used as an infallible criterion to mark off truth from falsehood, right from wrong. The first of these supposed infallible authorities is the Catholic Church. To most Protestants the idea of an infallible Church is not easy to understand, but to a Catholic it appears simple and satisfying. It starts from the belief that Jesus Christ, when He chose and trained His Apostles, was deliberately founding a visible and permanent corporation to carry on His work—a body charged by God Himself with the function of saving men and teaching them what they ought to believe and do.   God Himself is in the Church, just as truly as He was in Jesus. The Church, indeed, continues the Incarnation, which is thus, especially in the Sacraments, brought close to us, and is not an event of the past alone. God being thus incarnated in the Church, she is by her very nature infallible ;   otherwise God Himself would be guilty of error or deception.

But of whom does the Church consist ? There are two definitions, a smaller and a larger : the first is " *ecclesia docens* (the teaching body, *i.e.* the Apostles, and the bishops and priests who are their successors)" ; the second is " *ecclesia discens* (the learners, *i.e.* the general body of the faithful)." [1] It should be noted that the definition has nothing to do with inward and personal experiences like repentance and conversion ; for a " visible " Church must be defined by outward marks that are manifest to all.   The Church, in the Catholic idea, may have rebellious subjects, just as a State may ; but a baptized person, however sinful or unbelieving, is and remains a child of the Church until cut off by formal excommunication.

From the above definition it will be inferred, correctly, that Authority resides not in the Church in the larger sense but in the hierarchy : it is the Authority which Jesus Christ is supposed to have

[1] *Encylopædia of Religion and Ethics*, art. " Church (Roman Catholic)," Vol III, p. 629.   This is why churches are built with a " choir " separated from the rest of the church by a railing and steps. The " choir " is the priests' church, the rest that of the worshippers as a whole.

conferred upon His Apostles, a supernatural gift which they in turn conveyed by the laying on of hands to the Bishops, which has come down the line of Bishops in unbroken succession, and is by them communicated in measure to the clergy who have been " validly " ordained.   But how is it exercised, and who pronounces the final verdict in cases where lesser authorities disagree ?   Three answers have been given to this important question :   first, that it is a General Council of the Bishops ;   second, that it is the Pope ;   and third, that it is in the agreement of these two, the Pope and the Council.   At the present day, however, only one of these answers has a living interest.   For, in 1870, the Vatican Council declared that final infallibility, in matters of faith and morals, is vested in the Pope alone—and thereby signed its own death-warrant.[1]

Fantastic as it seems to Protestants, the dogma of the Pope's infallibility is the logical outcome of the Catholic theory of Authority.   Without attempting the task of proving this in detail, we may take it as

[1] To avoid misunderstanding as to what is meant by the dogma of the Pope's infallibility, it may be well to quote the words of the Vatican Council :

" The Roman Pontiff, when he speaks *ex cathedra*, that is, when in the discharge of his office of Pastor and Doctor of all Christians, he defines, in virtue of his supreme Apostolic authority, a doctrine of faith or morals to be held by the Universal Church, is, through the Divine assistance promised him in Blessed Peter, endowed with that infallibility with which our Divine Redeemer willed that the Church should be furnished in defining doctrine of faith or morals ;   and therefore such definitions of the Roman Pontiff are irreformable of themselves and not in virtue of the consent of the Church."   Further, " the Vatican ' Constitution ' now clearly states that a General Council is not to be looked upon as an authority above the Pope and capable of revising his decisions." —*E.R.E.*, article cited above, p. 628.

certain that the Bishops assembled in 1870 held that this dogma formed, implicitly, a part of the " deposit " from the beginning. They believed that they were only making it explicit. And, further, it should be noted that, if the Pope is not infallible, the Council is not infallible either ; for in that case it has made a mistake in declaring him to be so. It is hardly too much to say that the dogma has destroyed the power that created it, and annihilated its own foundations ; it has made the whole idea of Church Authority one great *petitio principii*. The Catholic believes in the infallibility of the Pope because the Pope has pronounced himself infallible, and the Pope in such a matter cannot err. The position is strictly parallel to that of the Protestant who bases his belief in the infallibility of Scripture on the text " All Scripture is given by inspiration of God," or of the Mohammedan who trusts the Koran because it declares itself to be fully inspired by God.

If the idea of the Church's infallible authority is looked at in the cold light of history, it is found to be without foundation. There is nothing, in the recorded teaching of Jesus, that in the remotest degree foreshadows it—except the words reported (in Matt. xvi. 18, 19) to have been addressed to Peter : " Thou art Peter (the rock) and on this rock I will build my church." The words are not found in our two oldest authorities, Mark and " Q " (the supposed collection of sayings of Jesus), and they are under grave suspicion of having been inserted through ecclesiastical influences. There is no sign that they were known to any other New Testament writer. It is very unlikely that they represent a genuine saying of Jesus ; but, whether they do or not, the interpretation which made them the basis for the paramount authority of the Roman Bishop, as the successor of Peter, was strongly opposed by various leaders in the Church even in the second century.[1]

There is no evidence that Peter was ever Bishop of Rome ; indeed he hardly could have been, for Apostles were essentially itinerant, while bishops were resident. No single Bishop of Rome is mentioned in the Epistle to the Romans ; in the Acts of the Apostles (ch. xxviii) ; in the Epistle to the Philippians, written from Rome ; in the letter written by Clement of Rome, on behalf of the church there, to the Corinthians (about 95 A.D.) ; in that of Ignatius to the Romans, written before his martyrdom in 115 ; or in the *Shepherd* of Hermas, written at Rome probably near the end of the first century.[2] There does not appear to have been any single Bishop of Rome before the reign of Hadrian (117–138 A.D.), the varying lists of early bishops found in certain writings having been invented to prove a case. In Rome, as in other churches, the presbyters, elders or bishops, who were originally chosen by the congregation, gradually gained more and more authority, and their president eventually became " the bishop " *par excellence*. No bishops are mentioned in Paul's letters to the Corinthians ; had there been any in the Corinthian church, he would almost certainly have alluded to them when dealing with the need of conducting religious services in an orderly manner. The epistle of Clement to the church at Corinth was written to protest against disorders there, in which certain

[1] Tertullian, Origen, and even Cyprian. See A. Sabatier, *Religions of Authority*, etc., p. 119.

[2] For these writings see Lightfoot, *The Apostolic Fathers*.

persons had " made sedition against their presbyters," and apparently driven them out of office.[1] It shows the kind of conflict that arose in decadent churches between the presbyters, who were servants of the local community, and the " apostles, prophets and teachers " who were for the most part in the service of the Church at large. It was as the gifts of the latter declined, as the life of the Spirit grew feeble, as doubtful teaching and unhelpful " prophecy " began to manifest itself, that the demand for order in the Church developed the power of the bishop. As Christianity grew inwardly cold, the attempt was made to strengthen its external unity by a more closely-knit organization.

Church authority, therefore, as exercised through the bishops, indicates not the presence of the Spirit in the hierarchy but its decline in the Church at large. It means the displacement by a human organization of the free and spontaneous working of the Spirit which had characterized the early days ; it marks the coming to the front of the human and not the Divine element in the Church. In the third century the Montanists tried to throw off the yoke of the hier-archy, and revert to the earlier freedom of inspired prophecy. Unfortunately its worked-up fervours were not, for the most part, " in the life," and they tended, on the whole, to discredit prophecy and strengthen the demand for authoritative control.

Examination of the history of the Church during these early centuries reveals no such supernatural consistency and coherence, in the decisions of Councils and Popes, as the theory of infallible authority would require. The paramount authority of the Bishop of

---

[1] On this, see further p. 49.

Rome was only recognised after fierce conflicts with other bishops ; by the Eastern Church it has never been recognised at all ; but the same causes that pushed to the front the president of a local presbytery gradually transformed the Church at large from a democracy to a monarchy. And, as the Empire had its centre at Rome, it was natural that the Church should seek to model itself on the same pattern.

The history of the ecclesiastical monarchy is not dissimilar from that of any other. The most worldly weapons for acquiring and maintaining power were not despised. The " False Decretals " of the pseudo-Isidore, a series of apocryphal decisions by mythical Popes, became the foundation of Roman canon law and of the universal theocracy aimed at by Gregory VII and Innocent III. The declarations of various Popes, on matters regarded as of the essence of true Christian belief, show no such uniformity and consistency—with one another or even with themselves— as we must look for if they were infallible. Vigilius, who was Pope from 537–555 A.D., before his election to the See of Rome wrote to some " monophysite " bishops stating that he held their view (that Christ had a single and not a double " nature "), but that they were to keep this secret lest it should injure his candidature ; and after his election he more than once changed his view. Pope Honorius (625–638) was pronounced heretical and accursed by the sixth Ecumenical Council for holding the " monothelite " view that in Jesus there was only a single will.[1] It is perfectly clear to the unbiased student of history that the dogma of papal infallibility was an

---

[1] See Martineau, *Seat of Authority in Religion*, pp. 139–143.

afterthought—a theory, developed later, to account for the power which the Pope had actually gained.

What, moreover, are we to make of the Council of Constance, which cited three rival Popes to appear before it and deposed them all, electing a fourth ? Either it was acting with authority, or without. If with authority, it was superior to the Papacy, and the Pope therefore not infallible ; if without, Martin V was no Pope and there is a breach in the succession : the cardinals he created were illegitimate, and all Popes since his time invalidly elected. Where, again, do we find infallibility in the repeated decrees that insist on the reality of witchcraft, or in those that condemned the views of Copernicus and Galileo—decrees that the Church dares now neither to defend nor to withdraw ? The truth is clear, that the Church of Rome has made the same sort of mistakes into which every human institution is liable to fall, and that its infallibility can only be held by those who surrender themselves wholly to it, deliberately blinding their eyes to the obvious facts of history.

A very few words must suffice for a bare notice of "Modernist" Catholicism as it appears in such writings as those of Loisy and Tyrrell. These men, believing themselves to be true sons of the Church, abandon altogether the attempt made by orthodox Catholics to show that the dogmas of the Church have been held by her, at least in essence, from the beginning. They are radical critics of the Gospels, and the figure of Jesus Himself melts in their hands into little more than that of a deluded visionary. The Church, in their view, has developed out of the practical needs of men, and is free to declare whatever is necessary to its life. If we ask whether its dogmas are *true*, the answer is that the only Truth we can reach is that which " works," which satisfies our life-needs It seems clear that this position does not conserve Church authority at all, and we cannot wonder that the Roman authorities will have none of it. In the words of Dr. Inge :

" If it does not matter whether the Incarnation was a fact or a legend ; if Faith can create dogmas with the same freedom which Plato's Socrates claims in inventing his myths ; if things only exist as instruments for the will, and all events are plastic under the hand of the religious imagination ; we are transported into a world where there is no difference between fact and fiction, and where it is difficult to suppose that human conduct can matter much. Such a contempt for actuality is far removed from the Christian view of the world." [1]

If we turn for a moment to the more limited authority which is claimed for the Church by Anglicans, a measure of the same objection applies here as to the Roman view. The Anglican Church is essentially a compromise between Romanism and Protestantism, and nothing rigorous or severely logical can be expected from it. While there is much that is true and beautiful in the ideal of the Church as presented by some High Anglican writers like Dr. Gore, it is spoiled by the notion of the " Apostolical Succession," a dream as empty of historical reality as that of papal infallibility itself, and one which by denying the " validity " of Nonconformist orders and sacraments,

[1] Inge, *Faith and its Psychology*, p. 174. See also pp. 99–106.

is the fruitful parent of religious strife. The theory
is, of course, that the first Bishops were appointed,
by the laying on of hands, by the Apostles themselves,
and that the gift of authority so conferred has come
down in unbroken succession to the duly appointed
clergy ever since. But there is no historical evidence
that any Bishop in the Catholic sense was ever
appointed by an Apostle at all. The early presbyters
or " bishops " were, frequently at any rate, chosen by
the churches they were to serve. The *Didache*, or
" Teaching of the Apostles," a manual of church order
in use in some of the churches early in the second
century, says : " *Appoint for yourselves* therefore
bishops and deacons worthy of the Lord." Clement
of Rome, indeed, in his letter to the Corinthians to
which allusion has already been made, speaks of the
Apostles as appointing " their first-fruits to be
bishops and deacons," and of these as having been
" appointed by them (the Apostles), *or afterward by
other men of repute with the consent of the whole
Church.*"[1] This is the earliest allusion to appointment by the Apostles, and it seems to have been taken
at its face value by subsequent writers. But Clement
had a special reason for magnifying the authority of
the bishops (or presbyters) at Corinth whom he
considered to have been unjustly driven out, and he
seems to have generalised a method of appointment
which may (for anything we know) have been used
at Corinth, but which certainly was not universal.
He quaintly supports his contention by quoting Is. lx.
17 in the form " I will appoint their bishops in
righteousness and their deacons in faith." Elsewhere he takes for granted that a right-minded

[1] First Epistle of Clement, 42, 44.

" bishop " will retire of his own accord if he is not wanted by the Church.[1] His real view of Church authority is clearly democratic and not monarchical. The Anglican theory, though it can claim support from the writings of Fathers of the Church from Irenæus onward, will not bear historical investigation.

And yet, beneath all the extravagances and un-realities that have marked the Catholic notion of Church authority, there is at least this solid nucleus of truth : that the Holy Spirit of God is a present possession of the community of Christ's faithful followers, and that in the unity of the Christian consciousness there is an authority, not absolute and final, but real and living, which has its right place in correcting the vagaries of individual illumination. Each of us needs to " put himself to school within a larger religious experience than his own." We all require the wise leadership of those who are more highly endowed with the things of the Spirit. Most of us need advice and help, and often a measure of control, from persons wiser than ourselves. For such authority there is ample room in the Church of Christ ; and it was such authority that our Lord committed to His Apostles.

Whether He ever contemplated founding any such institution as the Catholic Church may well be doubted. What is certain is that He did not con-template setting up a despotic authority to rule

---

[1] First Epistle of Clement, 54 : " Who therefore is noble among you ? Let him say, ' If by reason of me there be faction and strife and divisions, I retire, I depart whither ye will, and *I do that which is ordered by the people* : only let the flock of Christ be at peace with its duly-appointed presbyters.' "

the lives and the minds of His followers. In our oldest Gospel He reproves two of His disciples for desiring to rule the rest, and tells them that " whoever would be first among you shall be the slave of all " (Mark x. 42–45). As reported in the first Gospel He goes further, and tells them that none of them is to be called Rabbi, or father, or master : " for one is your teacher, and all ye are brethren " (Matt. xxiii. 8–11). There is no room here for the Catholic notion of authority as committed to a line of bishops and clergy. The true Apostolic Succession, it has been well said, is not to be sought in the thin trickle of a line of bishops, but in the broad stream of a common Christian experience. The Spirit was meant to be the normal endowment of the whole Church. It did not leave the world of men when the last page of the Bible had been penned ; nor was it ever the monopoly of any priestly caste. In the primitive Church the gift of the Spirit, and this alone, made a person a member of the Christian community ; and whatever authority was recognised as pertaining to the Church had its seat in the full assembly of believers.

CHAPTER VI

THE AUTHORITY OF THE BIBLE

IT has often been said that, while Catholics find their ultimate authority in an infallible Church, Protestants try to discover it in an infallible Bible. Strictly speaking, this is not correct ; for, as will be noticed later, the official Protestant position has always been that we believe in the Bible because the Holy Spirit testifies to its truth. Yet in practice many Protestants have sought to find in the Bible the final and infallible authority in religion ; and so far their position does not differ in principle from that of Catholics. It is simply the substitution of one supposed infallibility for another. The Protestant who believes that a man was literally swallowed by a fish, and after three days cast out alive, simply because he finds such a statement in the Bible—and adds, perhaps, that if the Bible said Jonah swallowed the whale he would believe it—is in exactly the same intellectual place as the Catholic who believes that Mary was born sinless (the dogma of the " Immaculate Conception "), not because he discerns it to be true, but because the Church tells him it was so. In each case what is really believed in is not the statement but the authority that vouches for it.

In the conflict between the two authorities, the logical and spiritual advantage undoubtedly lies with the Catholic. For the Protestant, to state his position, has to mark off a certain set of religious books (the " canon " of Scripture) from a large number of others ; and to declare his belief that the first set are full of Divine inspiration and infallibility while the others are mere human writings. Now the only guarantee he has for making this sharp distinction is that these books have been pronounced to be author- itative by Councils of the very Church whose final authority he denies. And he is substituting, for an authority living and close at hand, able (so the Catholic believes) to guide in new conditions and answer new questions as they arise, an authority that is of the past alone, fixed in a volume of ancient writings that can never be altered or adapted.

In point of fact, few instructed Protestants have held, with rigorous logic, the position here described. Luther and the early Reformers were far indeed from so stultifying themselves. They had found for themselves a new standing before God, by coming (as they believed) into a direct and experimental relation with Jesus Christ, entirely apart from obedience to the authority of the Church. Luther, it has been said, re-discovered the worth of the individual, and raised him erect upon his feet in the very presence of God. The air that Luther breathed was that of inward, not outward, authority. Never a logical thinker, and often professing contempt for human reason, he constantly appealed to an inward witness, " the Testimony of the Spirit," deep in the heart of the individual, to guarantee the truth of Scripture itself. And he felt no necessity to accept the whole canon of Scripture to which the Church of Rome had set its seal. He criticized it with considerable freedom, excluding from the list of truly " inspired "

E

writings the book of Esther, as too much filled with "heathen naughtiness," and calling the epistle of James, since it did not seem to him to teach justification by faith in Christ, " a veritable epistle of straw." Calvin's position was similar to Luther's. He rejected the authenticity of the second epistle of Peter, which had with difficulty found its way into the canon, and never commented on the Book of Revelation.

Moreover, the Reformed Confessions of faith, while pronouncing the Scripture to be " the word of God," are careful to explain that it is to be received as such because of the inward witness of the Holy Spirit. For example, the Westminster Confession, after naming the traditional list of books, excluding the Apocrypha, and stating that " the authority of the holy scripture, for which it ought to be believed and obeyed, dependeth not upon the testimony of any man or church, but wholly upon God (Who is truth itself) the author thereof ; and therefore it is to be received, because it is the word of God," goes on to declare that " our full persuasion and assurance of the infallible truth and divine authority thereof, is from the inward work of the Holy Spirit, bearing witness by and with the word in our hearts." [1]

Unfortunately, the exigencies of the Reformed Churches were very pressing, and they never allowed the seeds of free and unfettered examination of the Biblical documents, which Luther dropped, to germinate and grow. They were faced on the one hand with the need of making good their position against the mighty Church of Rome, and on the other of countering the disintegrating tendencies of the Anabaptist and other " illuminate " movements

[1] *Westminster Confession*, sections IV and V.

which threatened to resolve the Protestant faith into anarchy and licence. And so the arguments of the Protestant leaders became more and more intellectual, and their conception of authority purely external. They took the fatally easy path of identifying, as Luther had never done, the canonical Scriptures with the " word of God " that was in them, and, while professing that the Holy Spirit assured them of the infallible truth of these writings, devoted all their energies to the vain attempt to prove the position by argument. The result was a " Protestant Scholasticism," a desert of sophistication, in which the pure water of the revelation of God contained in the Bible was well-nigh swallowed up and lost. It is probably this, more than any other cause, that explains the Catholic reaction of the early seventeenth century, when, in several of the European countries, nearly everything was lost that Protestantism seemed to have gained.

There, is indeed, a flagrant lapse of logic in the assumption that the inward witness of the Spirit will necessarily guarantee the " inspiration " of precisely those books which the Church tradition has handed down. This has always been one of the inherent weaknesses of the orthodox Protestant position. The history of the canon is obscure ; but a very little study will convince anyone that it is quite impossible to separate by any rigid division the " inspired " books from the rest. The Church of Rome had in some measure recognised that " inspiration " is a matter of degree. She had a secondary list of books, which had been accepted by the Jewish authorities at Alexandria, though not by the stricter Jews of Palestine, known as the Apocrypha, which she regarded as in some degree inspired. The Reformers rejected them. But they never explained how it was that the Holy Spirit showed them that all the books in the main list were full of Divine authority, while none in the second list possessed it. It is not too much to say that no man's "inward witness" assures him that every word in Ecclesiastes or Esther is inspired by God, while Ecclesiasticus and the Wisdom of Solomon are mere human writings. If he makes any such sharp distinction, it can only be because he supposes there is some other authority, outside his own spiritual insight, which guarantees the first list but not the second. And, when closely examined, this "other authority" is found to reside in decisions of Jewish synagogues or rabbis, to whom, therefore, actually if unconsciously, some degree at least of infallibility is assigned. Similarly, the only ground for assigning plenary Divine authority to the second Epistle of Peter, and not to the newly-discovered "Odes of Solomon," is that the former was included in the canon of Scripture, in the fourth century, by a Council of the Catholic church—that Church whose final authority in other matters the Protestant rejects.

We may, indeed, be very thankful for the insight and sound judgment which, speaking broadly, were displayed by the Jewish and Christian authorities that selected the books to form the canon of the Old and New Testaments. They were undoubtedly successful in choosing those books that, on the whole, possessed the greatest religious value. Most of the books of the Apocrypha are at a lower level of inspiration than most of the books of the Old Testament ; and the difference is even more striking between the books that were selected for the New Testament and even the best of those that were refused—such as the Epistle of Clement, the Epistle of Barnabas, and the *Shepherd* of Hermas—to say nothing of the Apocryphal Gospels, which are mostly worthless. Yet one can only say " on the whole," because there are parts of some uncanonical writings which nourish the religious life better than some of the books included in the canon. And there is evidence that the selection was not infrequently based upon ideas of authorship which will not bear historical examination. Ecclesiastes and Canticles were almost certainly included because they were believed to have been written by Solomon ; 2 Peter because it claims his authorship ; and Hebrews because it was (quite wrongly) supposed to have been written by Paul. The last-named book is almost the only exception to the general rule that the books which were with most difficulty received into the canon of the New Testament were of less spiritual value than those which were readily accepted.

No thoughtful Protestant can now maintain, with any show of reason, that the Scriptures as we have them are the pure and unadulterated " word of God." Reserving for the moment a consideration of the results of criticism, we may see, in the light of a few general considerations, that the idea is frankly impossible. Let us grant at once that God is infallible, and assume that it is His will to reveal His truth to men. The inference that the Bible contains nothing but that truth, pure and unalloyed, involves not only Divine infallibility but four separate human infallibilities, not one of which is possible.

(*a*) It assumes that God's truth was infallibly *apprehended* by prophets and apostles and other Biblical writers—unless, indeed, it prefers to regard them, contrary to all evidence, as mere unconscious machines.

(*b*) It assumes that the truth, whether consciously apprehended or not, was infallibly *expressed* in human language.

(*c*) It assumes that the words so written have been infallibly *transmitted* to us.

(*d*) It assumes that we can infallibly *interpret* those expressions.

A very little thought will convince anyone that none of these human infallibilities does in fact exist.

(*a*) The Biblical writers show the clearest evidences of partial and not complete enlightenment. This is positively taught by our Lord in the Sermon on the Mount (Matt. v. 21 and *ff.*). The author (or authors) of the later part of the book of Isaiah—truly inspired, if anything in the Bible is so—attributed human sin to Jehovah (Is. xlv. 7, lxiii. 17). Paul definitely expected that, in his own lifetime, Jesus would appear again in glory (1 Thess. iv. 15–17). On the assumption that the authors were simply writing by Divine dictation, these mistakes would have to be assigned to God Himself.

(*b*) The idea that Divine truth could ever be expressed infallibly in human words can only be held by those who have never properly considered what language is. Missionaries to the heathen often find that there is no word in the native language to express what they want to say ; and all human language is, in like manner, in some degree inadequate. All the words by which we try to express the deeper realities of life are metaphors, derived from our sensuous experiences : spirit is " breath," existence is what " stands out," substance what " stands under," and so forth. Hence any form of words, applied to spiritual things, can do no more than *suggest* a great deal that words can never fully express. Words are nothing more than attempts to convey to others ideas and experiences ; how much they are able to convey depends upon the ideas and experiences of the society in which they pass current ; and, as this develops, the meanings of words alter. Hence, to speak of any infallible revelation in human language is absurd.

(c) The least study of manuscripts, or even of the Revised Version, shows at once that the words of the Biblical writers have not been infallibly transmitted to us. The existing MSS. show many thousands of variations ; and, though by textual criticism it is possible in many cases to get nearer to the original reading, in some this is gone beyond recall. Nor can it be said that these variations concern only minor details, and touch no important article of Christian belief. From 1 John v. 7, 8, certain very important words are omitted in the Revised Version, without a word of marginal explanation : " . . . in heaven, the Father, the Word, and the Holy Ghost, and these three are one. And there are three that bear witness in earth . . ." The fact is that these words were found only in Latin versions, and were not present in any Greek text earlier than about the fourteenth century. In the case of the Old Testament, there is evidence that, at a certain point in its history, the problem of variant readings was simplified by the expedient of selecting one type of MS. and destroying all the variants from it. Consequently, though in our Revised Version of the Old Testament far fewer differences of reading are noted in the margin than in the New Testament, the process of restoring the true text is far more difficult and in many cases impossible.

(*d*) Infallible interpretation is as impossible as infallible expression. As we have seen, words can do no more than *suggest* much that can never be fully expressed by them ; and what they suggest will depend in large measure on the experience of the reader. " God is love " means little or much to us, according to the poverty or richness of our experience of what love is. " The Devil," to a mediæval person, suggested a material being, black in colour, with horns and a tail. It does not suggest that to us. And, in very many cases, the meaning of Biblical passages is really doubtful. " Lovest thou me more than these ? " may mean, grammatically, in Greek as well as in English, " more than thou lovest these," or " more than these love me." The very important question whether Paul ever identifies Jesus Christ with God depends on the punctuation (and there were no stops in the oldest Greek MSS.) of Rom. ix. 5, " who is over all, God blessed for ever "—as may be seen from the margin of the Revised Version. It has been said that there are between 200 and 300 possible interpretations of Gal. iii. 20, " Now a mediator is not a mediator of one, but God is one." The science of Biblical exegesis is the endeavour to discover, with all the light that textual and historical study can supply, what the writers of the Bible had in their minds and wished to express ; and to put ourselves at their point of view so that we may be able sympathetically to explain their meaning.   This science, though a measure of agreement is happily being reached among competent students, is still very far from complete ; and so long as each reader, without the necessary knowledge, tries to interpret at his own sweet will, we can see the necessity, which the Catholic is never weary of urging, for an infallible interpreter to put us right.

If we insist on making the Bible an infallible outward authority, we cannot stop there, but must go on to the Catholic doctrine of an infallible Church. Happily, there is no need to take up any such dangerous and impossible position.   It was shown in the last chapter that the demand for infallible authority in the early Church was only felt as its spiritual life began to wane ; and it was so after the great revival which we call the Reformation.   So long as the glow of a new spiritual experience, in direct contact with the Spirit of Christ, was felt in the heart, its light shone upon the pages of Scripture, and simple souls found their needs were satisfied without any dogma of infallibility.   The inward Authority was felt to be sufficient, and this some of the early Reformers (at times at any rate) were prepared to admit.   Calvin held, says Sabatier, that " truth makes itself directly recognised as such by its intrinsic character, as things black and white reveal their colour to the eyes, and things sweet and bitter reveal their flavour."   " Only pious hearts know this," wrote Zwingli, " for faith does not depend upon the discussions of men, but has its seat, and rests itself invincibly, in the soul.

It is an *experience* which every one may have. It is not a doctrine, a question of knowledge, for we see the most learned men who are ignorant of this thing which is the most salutary of all."[1]   If only the later leaders of the Reformed Churches had followed this guidance, instead of squandering their souls in the barren wastes of intellectual sophistication, what troubles they might have spared the Protestant world !

So far, the Authority of the Bible has been dealt with apart from any consideration of what we mean by its Inspiration, and of the extent to which our ideas of inspiration have been affected by modern Criticism, whether textual or historical or literary.   These matters must now be very briefly considered, and we shall then be in a position to estimate what the Authority of the Bible really is, and how we ought to use it.   It will be well to take the second subject first.[2]

Criticism is simply the application to the Bible of common-sense methods of study—the same, precisely, that have to be used in the case of any ancient literature whatever.   We have already noted the necessity of Textual Criticism, to get back as nearly as possible to what was originally written.   It consists chiefly in comparing the common text with the oldest accessible MSS., with ancient versions, and with quotations found in early writers.   In these ways mistakes that have arisen through faulty copying, or through mistaking an explanatory note for part of the text, can often be corrected.   But Textual Criticism

---

[1] Quoted by A. Sabatier, *Religions of Authority*, p. 163.

[2] In what follows, occasional use has been made of some passages in the author's book, *The Bible, its Nature and Inspiration*.

inevitably leads up to what is unfortunately known as " Higher " Criticism—the purpose of which is to ascertain as nearly as possible when and by whom a book or a passage was written, and what were the circumstances that called it forth—that we may be able to place it properly, to appreciate the intention of the writer, and to judge how far he was well-informed. It is quite impossible to stop at Textual Criticism, the necessity of which every intelligent person understands, and to refuse to go on to the other. If, for example, we look at the beginning of John viii. in the Revised Version, we shall see that twelve verses, containing the wonderful story of the woman taken in adultery, is placed in brackets and separated by spaces from the rest. The margin tells us that " most of the ancient authorities omit " this passage, and that " those which contain it vary much from each other." It is certainly not an original part of the Gospel attributed to John. We cannot possibly help asking where it came from, who wrote it, and is it likely to be a true narrative ? That is " Higher Criticism."

Unless we imagine that there was no progress in Divine revelation, and that the truths declared in the New Testament are to be found in any part of the Bible—which is contrary to common sense and to the clear teaching of Jesus Himself—we are bound to try to ascertain the stages by which truth was revealed. And this means that the dates of the different books, and of important passages in the books, must be made the subject of careful enquiry ; otherwise we shall not be able to place them in any kind of historical sequence. There is much in the books themselves that may give a clue, even to an English reader who knows nothing of the original languages, to their approximate date. If, for example, we are asking whether Moses wrote the Pentateuch, we may light on such a passage as Gen. xxxvi. 31 : " These are the kings that reigned in the land of Edom, before there reigned any king over the children of Israel " ; and we are bound to ask ourselves whether this does not indicate that this part of the book at any rate was written for people who were already acquainted with Hebrew kings—which of course the men of the days of Moses were not. If a multitude of passages, and a careful study of the structure of the books, point to a date much later than the time of Moses, we may have to make up our minds that the traditional view of the Mosaic authorship of the Pentateuch must be abandoned.

Such study, carried on with the desire, not to " pull the Bible to pieces," but to understand what it really teaches, has convinced nearly all serious students in the present day that many traditional views concerning the date and authorship of Biblical books are not correct. It enables us, for example, to state with very strong probability that the " Book of Isaiah " was not all written by the prophet and statesman of the days of Hezekiah, about 700 B.C., but includes prophecies by various writers extending over a period of some 300 years. It leads us to the belief that many of the beautiful Psalms attributed to David (about 1000 B.C.) were really written long after his time. In the case of the New Testament, while at present it supports the traditional view that the third Gospel and the Book of Acts were written by Luke the companion of Paul, it makes it very hard to believe that the Pastoral Epistles were really the work of Paul, and as certain as any such judgment can be that the Epistle to the Hebrews was not. It raises grave doubts whether the fourth Gospel, with its marvellous picture of Jesus as the incarnation of the Divine Logos, can really have been written by the Galilean fisherman John the son of Zebedee—whether " the beloved disciple," on whose recollections the book professes to be based, was not someone else.

So critical study, which is a product of the last hundred years or so, has revolutionised many of the thoughts about the Bible which were held unquestioningly by the best-informed Christians before the nineteenth century. And this inevitably raises the question of Biblical Inspiration. What do we mean by the Inspiration of the Bible, and could an inspired writer make mistakes ? Could he hold erroneous views about matters of fact or history, and imperfect ideas even about the character of God and His will for men ? We must not close the question by a negative answer, as many of our forefathers did, assuming that anyone who is inspired by God is also infallible. For this is to impose on the Bible an idea of our own, which may not be true at all. Our view of Inspiration must grow out of our study of the Bible itself, it must be based on the facts we find there. This is the method which the modern or " scientific " spirit demands in all branches of enquiry. Reverence for facts is its keynote. It is the path of real humility. We must not attempt to tell God how He ought to reveal Himself to men ; we must be willing to learn how He has actually done so. We have to *find out* what the Inspiration of the Bible is, from the study of the Bible ; there is no short cut to a ready-made definition of it. It is impossible here to enter on a full discussion of the subject ; two points alone can be considered.

First, the Inspiration of the Bible is something we have to recognise for ourselves. It has meaning for us as we come to perceive and feel it—just as the beauty of a great picture, or the power of a great poem, must be felt and perceived by ourselves if for us it is to be a reality. Every rightly-constituted mind feels the beauty and power of the twenty-third psalm, or of the noble hymn concerning Love in 1 Cor. xiii. We discern freshness and a vital spiritual quality in the great utterances of psalmists, prophets and apostles, and most of all in the teaching of Jesus Christ. When, for instance, we come across a great saying like that of Micah. vi. 8, " What doth the Lord require of thee but to do justly, and to love mercy, and to walk humbly with thy God ? "—and recognise that it was a judgment not derived from antiquity or from current religious opinion, but one that sprang up as a new and certain truth in the soul of the prophet himself—and when we ask how it came there, the only natural and satisfying answer, if we believe in God at all, is that it was a truth revealed to the prophet by the Spirit of God, who gave him power to express it. It is not in the least necessary that it should have been uttered by him in a condition of trance or ecstasy in which he was a passive or unconscious instrument in the hands of God. It is just as truly inspired if the prophet was master of all his faculties, and if his ordinary powers were raised to a new level of insight and expression by the Divine Spirit working in him. Nor is it at all necessary that he should have been incapable of making mistakes, either as to matters of fact or of

God's ways of dealing with men. In any case the inspiration is *there*, and any sympathetic and spiritual mind can feel it. That is inspired which is truly and lastingly inspiring.

But, secondly, the Bible contains a great deal of matter that does not carry its own evidence of inspiration ; and yet we are told that the whole of it is inspired. There is a real sense in which we can rightly hold it to be so. What we have to lay hold of is a thread that runs all through it, and connects together its least impressive parts with those that move and inspire us. That thread is to be found in the conviction, with which the open-minded study of the Bible leaves us, that it is the record of *a great Divine process* by which the minds and souls of a portion of the human race were gradually prepared to receive a fuller manifestation of God—a process which culminated in the person and work of Jesus Christ. The Bible is man's record of this gradual process of revelation, it is not the revelation itself. We cannot find in it a final and infallible standard of truth or duty. It is indeed full of God, and in a real sense it all points to Christ, who is the expression of God in terms of humanity ; but, being man's record, it is full of imperfections. We cannot use it *mechanically*, when we seek in it guidance on our problems, as though all parts of it were on one level of Divine infallibility. It contains no single and uniform answer to any of the great questions we may ask. But it does lead us to Jesus Christ, to an understanding of the need of the human soul for His revelation of God, to a realisation of what His first followers found in Him.

The modern method of studying and using the

Bible does not set aside its legitimate Authority ; what it does is to help us to understand that the Bible is, next to Jesus Christ Himself, the greatest outward authority that has been given to men, because it records the profoundest religious experiences through which man has passed, culminating in that of the Son of Man.   But the foundation of its authority is inward, not outward ; it rests in the appeal to a witness of truth in our own hearts.   " For the letter killeth ; it is the Spirit that giveth life."

CHAPTER VII

THE AUTHORITY OF JESUS CHRIST

CHRISTIAN experience testifies to the power of the Scriptures to become the channel through which the life of God can reach and vivify human hearts. The Inward Witness testifies to the moral beauty, the soul-reaching and heart-cleansing power, of the revelation of God that is their central theme. Religious experience in ourselves, as it deepens and broadens, verifies more and more the progressive religious experience of which the Scriptures contain the record and the expression. The Spirit within us answers to the Spirit without us, deep calls to deep.

But this must not blind us to the fact that the books of the Bible are human documents, each of which has had its human history. As we have seen, those Protestants were guilty of grave confusion of thought, who tried to use the Inward Witness as a substitute for knowledge of history. We cannot appeal to it for evidence that Moses wrote the Pentateuch, or that " the disciple whom Jesus loved " was John the brother of James. Religious experience and insight is, indeed, an indispensable qualification for a sympathetic understanding and exposition of what the Biblical writers had to say ; but, taken alone, it cannot possibly inform us how far their words have

F

been correctly transmitted, when they lived, what were their circumstances and their modes of thought, whether their writings are to be understood as history, or parable, or poetry, or what degree of credence is to be attached to their statements of fact. For all these things we must use our independent powers of enquiry and historical and literary judgment, and we must use them unhampered by conceptions of authority. The truth, and nothing else, must be both goal and guide.

There are some who fancy that this labour may be spared by an appeal to the authority of Jesus Christ. While admitting, it may be, that neither Church nor Bible is in itself the ultimate court of appeal, such Christians would try to reinstate one or both by basing their authority on recorded words of Jesus. The Catholic appeals to his words to Peter as implying that to him, and to his supposed successors as Bishops of Rome, plenary authority was committed. The Protestant, in the same manner, often quotes His recorded utterances in regard to Noah, Jonah, Isaiah, or Daniel—or His apparent recognition of the Davidic authorship of a certain psalm (Mark xii. 36) —as settling, without labour of historical investigation, any question that might arise about them. The words about the law of Moses attributed to Jesus in the Sermon on the Mount (Matt. v. 18) are sometimes quoted as if they guaranteed the absolute Divine inerrancy of the Old Testament as we have it. The argument is that since Jesus was Divine He must have known all about these matters, and therefore enquiry is superfluous and even impious ; it implies doubt or disbelief in His Divine knowledge.

And what of passages like Matt. vii. 28 (Mark i. 22)

—" the multitude were astonished at his teaching : for he taught them as one having authority, and not as their scribes " ? Does not this imply that His hearers must accept His word as Divine and therefore unquestionable ? The answer is that, if we look at the Gospels broadly, we shall certainly conclude that His " authority " does not mean this. He con- stantly appeals to a witness within the souls of His hearers which, if they attend to it, must convince them that what He says is true. " Why even of yourselves judge ye not what is right ? " He says, in Luke (xii. 57), just as in the fourth Gospel He is represented as saying, " If I say truth, why do ye not believe me ? " (John viii. 46). This can only mean that He said things because they were true, and that His hearers could perceive this if they would— not that things must be taken as true because He said them. His " authority " is that which always accompanies the sense that a man is speaking of what he knows. Jesus simply declares what He can see to be the truth ; He does not try to prove it, like a philosopher, nor does He base it, like the scribes, on what others have said in the past. Even in the " But I say unto you " of the Sermon on the Mount, He is appealing to the inward authority in men's souls, and not seeking to suppress it by His own personal claim. When challenged by His adversaries to produce His credentials, giving Him authority to act as He had done in the Temple, He silenced them by asking in reply what were the credentials of John the Baptist—implying that in both cases they knew in their own hearts that the authority was from God. (Mark xi. 27–33).

The question, however, of His use of the Old

Testament is serious, because His authority is often appealed to in order to maintain positions that free investigation has rendered untenable. It is strange that Christians who are really loyal to their Master can put Him into such a place of danger ; it can only be because they do not know, and are unwilling to ask or to face, what the evidence really is. To say that, if Jesus Christ is Divine and therefore trustworthy, Moses must have written the Pentateuch and David the 110th Psalm, is to put Him at the mercy of the first critic who shows the contrary. And this contrary has, by cumulative evidence, been raised to such a degree of probability as to have convinced nearly everyone whose mind is open to the facts. Without subscribing to any wild theories of a merely " subjective " and arbitrary criticism, every unbiased student now recognises that there is a substantial body of real knowledge, gained by the patient labours of critics and archæologists, concerning the history of Old Testament documents, and that in the light of this knowledge many traditional views about them can no longer be held as true. It is the very opposite of a service to Christian faith to invoke the authority of Jesus Christ in order to disprove the results of scientific study. One would have supposed that the Church's condemnation of Galileo would have been warning enough that the mistake should not be repeated.

Moreover, this use of the authority of Christ involves a vicious circle akin to that which we have noticed in the attempt to prove the Bible from the miracles and the miracles from the Bible. We try to use the words of Jesus to prove the authorship of Old Testament documents ; but how do we know that we have really got His words ? The answer " because they are recorded in the Bible " assumes the very point at issue—whether the Bible is or is not inerrant and infallible. Criticism is applied to the New Testament documents as well as to the Old ; and it shows us, with strong probability, that the earliest record we have of Jesus was not compiled till many years after his death, when those who had known Him in the flesh were passing away. Our oldest Gospel, that of Mark, can hardly have been written before 65 A.D., a generation after His crucifixion ; the supposed collection of " sayings," known as Q, which is freely used by " Matthew " and Luke, may have been compiled rather earlier. The other Gospels are almost certainly much later. The words of Jesus were not written down, as we now have them, till they had passed through a considerable time of oral tradition ; and, while we are right in recognising their very impressive quality, and the retentiveness of the oriental memory, there is no certainty that we have got His exact words before us. Comparison of the same saying in different Gospels (for example Matt. v. 3 with Luke vi. 20) shows how freely His sayings were rendered, how far from rigid was the form in which they were repeated. While for the most part we can trust the general sense, we cannot rightly press the precise words as recorded in any single Gospel. There is reason to believe, especially when passages in the Gospels are compared with quotations in early Christian writers, that even important doctrinal passages have been expanded by the authors of the Gospels, especially the first, in accordance with views of their own ; or have even been interpolated by later hands.[1]   Hence we must beware of pressing the letter of our Lord's recorded utterances, or of making much depend upon their verbal form.

It may seem to some that to admit any criticism of the Gospels must end in dissolving away the figure of the Lord into pure subjectivity.   But we cannot possibly escape it, if we even begin the work of comparing one Gospel with another.   And these doubters surely forget that behind all criticism stands *the great Fact* which neither tradition nor criticism can make or alter.   And what reverent criticism has done and is still doing is to bring us nearer to the Fact as it was : to the mind and character, the gracious and luminous personality, of the Lord of Life Himself.

" That one Face, far from vanish, rather grows,
    Or decomposes but to recompose."

But the centre of the difficulty has not yet been reached.   If criticism shows us that some of the statements attributed to Jesus, and which He probably really made, are unbelievable, what becomes of His authority ?   Does it not lead us to a direct denial of His Divine nature ?   Is not Christian faith attacked at its very heart ?   To answer such questions requires a book rather than a few paragraphs [2] ;   here we can do no more than suggest the lines on which, it is believed, a satisfying answer may be sought.   After all that can be shaken by criticism has been put on one side, the unbiased study of the New Testament

[1] Especially Matt. xvi. 18, 19, and xxviii. 19.   The teaching on Judgment and the final punishment of the wicked is much more pronounced in the first Gospel than in the others.   See *The Lord of Thought* (Dougall and Emmet), Part II.

[2] The whole subject is excellently treated by Dr. Forrest in *The Authority of Christ.*

seems to leave us face to face with two unshakeable facts :

(1) The real though sinless humanity of Jesus.

(2) The fact that His followers, including those who had known Him as a friend and companion, began to speak of Him in terms of worship, as Lord and Saviour.

(1) The Gospel figure of Jesus, especially in our earliest Gospel, that of Mark, is of One who was truly human as we are, subject to weakness and limitation of power and knowledge, feeling the pull of real temptation to choose an easier path than that which He knew was marked out for Him, yet always over-coming it. The portrait, simple in its outlines and unadorned, is that of a man so perfect in character as to be also perfect in humility and self-surrender— and, as such, it is beyond invention by any power of human fancy. What we call His " sinlessness " is more than a fact, it is a Value, and is therefore incapable of formal proof. It is an essential part of our intuition of His character, and, as such, it is more certain than a fact proved by logical processes. We cannot prove the beauty of a landscape or a poem, we can only perceive it for ourselves. If any one does not perceive it, we can only be sorry ; it does not alter our certitude. But, although we cannot prove from our fragmentary records the sinlessness of Jesus, all the evidence we have supports our intuition. He overcame temptation with the same weapons that we have to use—prayer, faith, and absolute dependence on God. God was to Him what God is to the saintliest of men—only much more. That is doubtless why in the New Testament Jesus

is hardly ever, if ever, called simply " God." There have been grave dangers in doing this all through the history of the Church, and there are now. The danger is that the real impression He makes on us is apt to be quite blurred if we begin to argue that because He was " God " He was not compassed with our limitations—that He must have possessed all power and all knowledge, and could not really have been tempted like ourselves.

(2) But those whom Jesus rescued from sin and brought into a new life and fellowship with God could not rest till they called Him Lord, Saviour, Revealer— until they used about Him terms that had previously been applied to God alone. Peter, for example, (who, if he did not actually write, almost certainly stands behind, the first Epistle that bears his name) breaks out into a song of praise concerning " Jesus Christ, whose is the glory and the dominion for ever and ever " (1 Pet. iv. 11). It was in their hymns of praise that the early Christians could alone express what Jesus had become to them. " Dogma," says Dr. Rendel Harris, " begins in Doxology "; it hardens into dull prose what can only be expressed in song. It is the more remarkable that the first disciples of Jesus should have begun to worship Him as Divine, when we remember that they were not polytheists like the Greeks, but Jews, and therefore almost fanatical monotheists. The idea of a " second God " was entirely abhorrent to them. It was far more difficult for them to deify Jesus than it is for Hindus to begin to worship Mr. Gandhi as a " Mahatma " or almost Divine being.

These two facts of experience—the outer experience of the character and personality of Jesus, and the inner

experience of what He had done for their souls—
coupled with their assurance of His resurrection from
the dead—supply the basis on which the early disciples of Jesus erected the doctrine about His Divine
nature which we find in the Epistles and in the fourth
Gospel. The process by which they reached it is
obscure, and need not now concern us. It is important to remember that they never lost hold on His real
humanity. Some Christians in the second century
did so, and this (the " Docetism " of the Gnostic
thinkers) was the first serious " heresy " in the Church.
Christian thought, in its main stream, held fast to His
true humanity while yet regarding Him as in some way
within the circle of Divinity. Reflection must convince us that this involved certain assumptions,
either explicit or sub-conscious and implicit :

(a) They must have come to hold that there are
distinctions within the Divine nature which do not
impair the unity of God. For Paul there is only " one
God," yet within this unity there is room for the " one
Lord Jesus Christ, through whom are all things "
(I Cor. viii. 6). For the author of the fourth Gospel
the Logos who " became flesh " was from the beginning "with God (ὁ θεός) and was God (θεός)." These
distinctions, which are beyond the compass of human
thought, later Greek Christians called *hypostases*,
a word which most unhappily was translated into
Latin as *personæ*, whence it has come to us as the
" persons " of the Trinity. It never meant " persons "
in our modern sense—for which, indeed, the Greeks
had no proper word—it rather meant modes of
existence which are beyond our powers to conceive.

(b) They clearly also held, whether explicitly or
not, that it was not (to speak quite inadequately,

and indeed misleadingly—but words fail us here—)
the *whole* of the Divine nature, but some part or
aspect of it, one of the " hypostases," that became
man in Jesus Christ ; and that therefore the Incarnation involved God's self-limitation or self-sacrifice,
yet without making Him any less than God. He
who " was rich yet for our sakes became poor "
(2 Cor. viii. 9) ; though equality with God was within
His reach, He refused it, and " emptied himself,
taking on him the nature of a slave " (Phil. ii. 6, 7).
This " Kenosis," which must be recognised by anyone
who takes the Incarnation seriously, we can best
think of on ethical lines, as essentially the same in
nature as the self-sacrifice (which is also self-realisation)
involved in all true love and loving service. The
early Christian thinkers found in it the highest
manifestation of that Love which had always been
the Divine nature, which had always been pouring
itself out for men. " For no noble deed," says
Origen, " has ever been done among men, without the
Divine Logos visiting their souls." [1]

The significance of this brief enquiry into the earliest
Christian theology is this : that it helps us in some
measure to believe, though we can never fully understand, that in becoming truly man Jesus did not
cease to be Divine. In human love self-sacrifice
is the means to fuller self-realisation ; " he that
loseth his life shall save it." The higher self grows
and develops as the lower self is transcended by love.
May we not, with all reverence, think in this way even
of God Himself ? If we rightly hesitate to say that
the Incarnation made a difference to God, enabling

[1] *Contra Celsum*, vi. 78 *ff.* (abbreviated). Quoted by Hort, *Ante-
Nicene Fathers*, p. 133.

Him to understand and sympathize and enter into fellowship with men more fully than ever before, because even He had gained new experiences by it, at least we may say with confidence that it made a vast difference to God *as known to men*, that (in relation to us at least) He became more truly God.   And, the more completely He became one with us, bone of our bone and flesh of our flesh, the more abundantly His true nature was revealed.   The greater the humiliation, the greater was the love displayed.   " The Cross is the power of God."

If such thoughts are in the direction of the truth, then the authority of Christ as the eternal Word or Son of God is no other than the authority of God Himself, and is therefore final and absolute.   But it is not *outward* authority.   To find a final outward authority in Jesus Christ, we should have to attribute Divine infallibility to every word He is reported to have spoken in the body, and to every thought that passed through His human mind.   And this we cannot do without denying at once the imperfections of the record and the reality of the Incarnation.   If Jesus Christ was truly man, then His thoughts in the flesh were compassed with limitation.   A real man is one who learns, who grows, in mind as well as in body.   An omniscient baby would not be a human child.   Yet, if Jesus was not omniscient in His cradle, at what point did He become so ?

The Christian belief is that the Son of God, for our redemption from sin, submitted Himself to become one of ourselves.   He became, as the author of Hebrews says, our brother, " made in all things like unto his brethren " (Heb. ii. 17) : a real man, a real Jew, fulfilling indeed the highest of His people's yearnings, yet sharing their limitations. He seems to have known nothing of Greek literature and philosophy, or of Roman Law ; poetry and art and science were beyond His ken. But He was steeped, apparently from early youth, in His nation's sacred literature ; and, while transcending immeasurably the religious ideas of His time, He spoke, and doubtless thought, according to the fashion of His day. The scheme of the universe which His people held, He held also. To teach them a better astronomy was no part of the work He had come to do ; and literary and historical criticism lay equally outside His sphere. He took as He found them the prevalent ideas about the authorship of Old Testament books ; to have done otherwise would have hindered His purpose of revealing the Father and winning men from sin into the life of God. The more clearly we discern His purpose, and the more firmly we hold to it, the more unfettered will be our freedom of enquiry into matters of history.

The authority of Jesus Christ, the man of Galilee, differs not in nature but only in degree from that of all who can see more deeply than others into the truth of things. Everyone, as was said in the first chapter of this book, who has special first-hand knowledge on any subject, speaks about it with authority, and that authority we commonly recognise. The prophets and saints of humanity have authority when they tell us what they see of the deep things of God and of the spiritual life of man. Their authority is relative and partial, but it is none the less real. So the authority with which Jesus of Nazareth speaks of God, of sin, of forgiveness and of righteousness, is the outcome of that wondrous clearness of spiritual vision which shines everywhere on the Gospel pages, and which can only have been possible for One who lived ever in perfect communion with God. His authority covers the matters concerning which He had special knowledge, not those of which He had not. To quote His words in support of traditional theories about the Old Testament is to miss His true significance, to go back from the light and freedom of the Gospel to the darkness and bondage of the Scribes and Pharisees. He is our highest outward Authority in Religion ; but no outward authority can ever be final and absolute.

Admittedly the work of Christ was only begun, not finished, while He was here on earth. " I have yet many things to say unto you, but ye cannot bear them now. Howbeit when he, the Spirit of truth, is come, he shall guide you into all the truth " (John xvi. 12, 13). We hope in the next chapter to show how, through the Spirit, the authority of Christ became effective for the direction of His Church.

CHAPTER VIII

THE AUTHORITY OF THE SPIRIT

It has often been remarked that the Apostolic writers make surprisingly little use of the deeds or sayings of their Master. Whether we take the New Testament epistles, or the accounts of the earliest Christian preaching that appear in the Acts of the Apostles, the references to the acts or words of Jesus are remarkably few. Almost the only events in His career that are mentioned, apart from the general statement that He " went about doing good," are His birth into our human nature, His death for our sins, and the resurrection by which " life and immortality " were " brought to light." And very rarely are His teachings quoted even when we should expect them to be inevitably appealed to as the final court of reference. His first disciples certainly did not use His authority in the way that some modern Christians have tried to do.

This fact has been used to throw doubt upon the historical worth of the Gospel narratives, and even upon the real existence of Jesus Himself. It has been imagined, by John M. Robertson and others, that the rise of Christianity can be explained without a historic Founder, as the development of a Jewish cult of a dying and rising God. It seems needless to spend time on considering this speculation. We take it that anyone who in the least apprehends what sort of men the first Christians became, and the new religious experience that the New Testament discloses, must be convinced that without Jesus behind them these men are absolutely inexplicable—an event without a cause, a greater miracle than orthodoxy itself has dreamed of.

Nevertheless the fact is a strange one, and demands explanation. It is not enough to say, what is perfectly true, that when Paul wrote his epistles the Gospels as we have them were not compiled. For it is practically certain that, from the departure of Jesus, stories of His deeds, and reports of His sayings, were carefully taught in the infant Church and handed on from mouth to mouth. It is these that form the basis of our first three Gospels ; the material must have been at hand for Paul and others to use, had they so desired.[1]

The absence of reference to the Master's teaching is perhaps most striking in the settlement of the hardest question the first Christians had to face— the position of converted Gentiles in the new society, and the authority over them (and, indeed, over Christians generally) of the Mosaic law. The passages (not easily reconciled with one another) that throw most light on the acute controversy that arose about this question are Gal. i and ii and Acts xi. 1–18 and xv. 1–29. In the whole of this there is only one reference to any word of Jesus (Acts xi. 16).

No doubt, even if the disciples had wished to do so,

---

[1] In Acts xx. 35 Paul is reported as quoting from this floating tradition the saying (not elsewhere recorded), " It is more blessed to give than to receive." In 1 Cor. xi. 23–25 we have his only reference to an event in the life of Jesus (the last supper) other than the birth, death and resurrection. He introduces it by saying that he " received it from the Lord," but no one seems to know what this means.

it would not have been easy to settle their dispute by reference to the sayings of their Master. If the more liberal section quoted the prophecy that " Many shall come from the east and from the west, and shall sit down in the Kingdom of heaven " (Matt. viii. 11), the strict Jewish party could remind them of the words " I was not sent but unto the lost sheep of the house of Israel " (Matt. xv. 24). If some pleaded that Jesus had not practised any great strictness of Sabbatic observance, or pointed out the boldness with which, in declaring that " nothing from without can defile a man," He " made all meats clean " (Mark vii. 17- 19, R.V.), and so set aside much of the ceremonial law—others could remind them of the saying, " One jot or one tittle shall in no wise pass from the law, till all things be accomplished " (Matt. v. 18). His method of teaching was not one that conveniently lent itself to mechanical reference.

Nothing is more noteworthy than the contrast between the methods of these disciples and those of the Jewish scribes by whom in earlier life they had doubtless been taught. The scribes decided every question by quoting some authority—a precept in their sacred law, with the interpretation and applica- tion of it laid down by this Rabbi or that. The disciples of Jesus, while using with freedom the prophetic writings, hardly ever quote their own Master. For this there must be some reason, which is not fully explained by the occasional and often paradoxical character of His utterances. What it was may be gathered from the one quotation which Peter (as reported) did make in Acts xi. 16 : " *Ye shall be baptized with the Holy Ghost.*" It was because they had a present illumination that they did not need to seek it in the past ; because of their daily experience of a living and accessible Friend and Counsellor that they never cast back their eyes regretfully to the days when their Master had been with them in the body, as to a time when the will of God had been more clearly known.   Not once is there the heaving of the sigh,

> " But O for the touch of a vanished hand,
>   And the sound of a voice that is still."

What these first Christians refer to as their Authority is not the remembered or recorded words of Jesus, but the mind of the Spirit.   " It seemed good," they say, " to the Holy Ghost and to us " (Acts xv. 28). They are " forbidden of the Holy Ghost to speak the word in Asia " (xvi. 6).   And this experience of Divine control and direction by the Spirit was not confined to a favoured few ; it was the normal endowment of all who genuinely accepted Jesus Christ.   Indeed, it was this gift and nothing external, like the ceremony of baptism, that was regarded as constituting a person a Christian.   It was because the Holy Ghost had " fallen on " Cornelius and his friends that Peter judged them to be fit for baptism (Acts x. 44–48).   As Paul wrote later to the Romans, " As many as are led by the Spirit of God, they are sons of God " (Rom. viii. 14).[1]

In all ages the sorest of the inward problems that perplex the human spirit has been " the Silence of God."   The hunger of man for an authentic voice from heaven—for some clear knowledge of the hidden mind of God—is seen not alone in the resort, in ancient days, to inspired prophets and priests with their

[1] Compare Forrest, *Authority of Christ*, pp. 351–360.

G

Urim and Thummim, but in Delphic oracle and Roman augury, in magic and divination, in the persistent belief, wide as the human race, that certain persons have dealings with the unseen world. See how the first Christians believed that in their experience this world-hunger was satisfied.

In the Book of Acts the chief disciple of Jesus is represented as claiming the gift of the Spirit as evidence that the Messianic Age has dawned—for the prophecy of Joel has been manifestly fulfilled, that Divine inspiration shall no longer be the privilege of the few, but shall be poured out upon all flesh (Acts ii. 15–18). The gift of the prophet—direct access to God and clear intimations of His mind and will—had now been made the possession of servants and handmaidens, of every humblest believer in Jesus. *The Christian Church was founded as the Church of an inspired people.* But what was the Spirit that inspired them, how were its intimations received, and what was the nature of its authority ?

In the first place " the Spirit " was regarded as continuous with the source of inspiration of prophets and psalmists (Acts. i 16). It was the same as the Divine " Wisdom " which " from generation to generation passing into holy souls maketh men friends of God and prophets " (Wisdom vii. 27). It was the Divine power that filled the Master Himself (Acts x. 38), and with which He baptized His followers.[1]

But, in the second place, it was felt to be in some sense a *new* gift, being identified with His own personality, risen and exalted. " The Spirit was not yet," says the fourth evangelist, " because Jesus was

[1] John xx. 22. This is regarded by some as the Johannine version of what happened at Pentecost.

not yet glorified " (John vii. 39).   " I will not leave you orphans," he reports Jesus as saying, " I come unto you "—in the same breath as the assurance that " the Spirit of truth shall be in you " (John xiv. 16–18).   " They assayed to go into Bithynia, but the Spirit of Jesus suffered them not " (Acts xvi. 7).[1]

The two thoughts of the Spirit as continuous, and of the Spirit as a new gift, were harmonized in the Johannine theology by the doctrine of the Word made flesh—which, though the term " Logos " is not used, is suggested in some of Paul's Epistles and in that to the Hebrews.   The eternal Logos had always been with men as a " life " in which they found their " light," a " light that lighteth every man."   But now, in the last days, this diffused light had been, as it were, focussed and concentrated into the clear beam of the person of Jesus Christ.   He had left this world in the body, but returned to it as the Spirit— no longer, as in former days, a dimly perceived influence, but recognised now as a personal presence having a definite mind and will, which, though it is identified, of course, with the mind and will of God,[2] is yet the same living and active personality who, as Jesus of Nazareth, had lived and died for men.

This consciousness of the presence and activity of the living Christ, the Spirit, is the most distinctive

[1] While, as was shown in the last chapter (p. 77), the Christian leaders were very early driven by their experience of Jesus as Revealer to assume some inconceivable distinctions within the Divine unity, they certainly had not in Apostolic days reached any formulated conception of a " Trinity," and we only misunderstand them if we suppose them to have distinguished in thought the living Christ as one " Person " and the Spirit as another.   Note Rom. viii. 9, 10, and 2 Cor. iii. 17, 18.

[2] Note that in the Johannine discourses of John xiv–xvi the Spirit begins to be spoken of as not " it " but " he " (ἐκεῖνος).

mark of primitive Christianity. It satisfied the human hunger for a God who is not " silent." It brought Divine authority close home to the minds and souls of men. The authority of Christ was not to be sought by any mechanical reference to the letter of His words on earth, but by seeking and following the teaching of His Spirit in the heart. The first followers of Jesus do not appear to have regarded the presence and guidance of the Spirit as something wholly " miraculous " or supernatural, whose working would be hindered by the use of their ordinary faculties of reason and judgment. It was largely through the right use of those faculties that the Spirit taught them—largely from facts and circumstances that they gathered what the mind of the Spirit was.

Chief among these new facts was one that greatly disconcerted them—the evidence that their Master was at work in the souls of men outside the artificial enclosure of Jewish law and practice. They had their choice to open their minds to these new facts, or to close them and continue in the old narrow groove. Happily for the world they chose the better path, submitted themselves to the facts, and found their hearts enlarged and their spiritual vision cleared. Their own inward experience was verified and enlarged through the evidence of changed lives all around them, in the fellowship of those who, though not Jews like themselves, were walking in the light.

" We have here " (says Dr. Forrest) " a classical illustration of what is meant by the illumination of the Spirit, and of the methods of His operation. In their whole action the one concern of the Apostles was to be loyal to the purpose of their Master.

They had the most vivid recollection of the time when He was with them, and of the teaching that He had imparted to them.   But where His word or example was insufficient for present guidance they never doubted that fresh light would break for them.   They found the sure indications of His mind through submitting themselves to His discipline of their life.   What they had imagined to be primary or essential in His utterances or acts, they now perceived to be subordinate or temporary. They read His declarations with a new accent or emphasis ; and they did so confidently, because it was still He who was teaching them by His Spirit." [1]

It was not only the collective Church that was thus taught by the Spirit.   The foundation of collective guidance lay in the measure of individual guidance known by each true Christian, however humble. " The young men saw visions, and the old men dreamed dreams."   Yet this made none of them infallible, " not even the youngest."   They record, in the frankest manner, their disagreements.   Paul reproached Peter at Antioch, " because he stood condemned " when he had not the courage of his convictions about eating with the Gentile Christians ; and quarrelled with his beloved Barnabas on the question of a companion.   He gave up his confident belief in the early return of his Master, yet never doubted that he had had the Spirit.   He frequently,

---

[1] Forrest, *The Authority of Christ*, pp. 360, 361.   The example here cited is of great importance at the present time, in relation to current proposals for " the Reunion of Christendom."   Any such proposal that leaves out a section of those who manifestly have the Spirit stands condemned.

in his writings, warns his readers against the spirit of infallibility, which has wrecked so many Christian societies ; and he does this usually in close connection with assurances of the plenitude of the Spirit's power. If his readers were to be "filled unto all the fulness of God," they must also " walk in all lowliness and meekness, forbearing one another in love " ; if " filled with the Spirit," they must yet " subject themselves one to another in the fear of Christ " (Eph. iii. 14–iv. 4, v. 18–21). Inspired preachers at Corinth must keep themselves under control, and be willing to yield one to another, that all things might be done decently and in order (1 Cor. xiv. 29–33).

The authority of the Spirit, then, as Paul conceives it, is the authority of the living Christ, present and available for all His sincere, obedient and humble followers. But the Spirit is not something wholly miraculous, wholly foreign to their own true nature, which makes any of them into infallible oracles of God. It is, in truth, their own best nature. God in them is the fulfilment of the best they have it in them to become. The higher nature begotten in them is " the first-fruits of the Spirit," with promise of ever richer fruition. The " groanings which cannot be uttered," with which the Spirit " comes in on our behalf," are identical with the groanings that we ourselves utter in the longing for a fuller experience of God (Rom. viii. 23–27).

In a previous chapter[1] it was noted how, in the history of the Church, as the free spontaneous life of the Spirit died away, and the consciousness of the

[1] Chapter V, p. 45.

present authority of the living Christ grew feeble, the demand arose that order and unity should be preserved through increasing the authority of the bishops, and building up an institutional religion based on rigid creeds and valid sacraments. Allusion was made to the unsuccessful attempt of the Montanists to throw off the yoke of the hierarchy, and return to the freedom of personal inspiration. As the centuries went by, other similar movements arose in the Church in which the attempt was made from time to time to restore " the authority of the Spirit " as it had been known in the earliest days. Only one of these has produced a society vigorous enough to last to our own day[1]—the Quaker movement of the seventeenth century. It is worth while to give a little space to this, since it illustrates a point of great importance in relation to the subject we are considering.

The Quaker movement arose out of the spiritual struggles of a half-educated lad, George Fox, who about the year 1647 met with an inward experience that transformed his life. From a despairing " Seeker " he became, without any human help, a happy " Finder " ; and he was able to bring many others into the same experience. He concluded that the Light from God that had arisen in his own soul was available for every man who would turn to it and obey it—that it was not the prerogative of any favoured few.

" Now the Lord opened to me by his invisible power that every man was enlightened by the

[1] The Franciscan movement of the early thirteenth century was soon so entirely transformed that it can hardly be regarded as contradicting this statement.

Divine Light of Christ ; and I saw it shine through all ; and that they that believed in it came out of condemnation to the light of life, and became the children of it ; but they that hated it, and did not believe in it, were condemned by it, though they made a profession of Christ. This I saw in the pure openings of the light, without the help of any man ; neither did I then know where to find it in the Scriptures, though afterwards, searching the Scriptures, I found it. For I saw, in that Light and Spirit which was before the Scriptures were given forth, and which led the holy men of God to give them forth, that all must come to that Spirit if they would know God, or Christ, or the Scriptures aright." [1]

The " Children of the Light " whom Fox gathered, not to himself but to Christ as their Leader, and who afterwards took the name " Society of Friends," repeated many of the features of primitive Christianity. They had only the simplest possible organization, with no separated clergy, no pre-arranged order of worship, no sacramental observances, and no formal creed. Every member, man or woman, was a potential recipient of the Spirit, and might share (if the inward call was felt to be a real one) in the vocal ministry. The meetings for worship were held in preliminary silence to allow freedom for such individual guidance. The fact that a body should have survived when built on the foundation of such personal freedom is a tribute, first to the reality of its Christian experience, and second to the sobriety of Fox's character, his profound ethical sense, and

[1] Fox's *Journal*, Bicentenary Edition, Vol. I, pp. 34, 35.

the skill he showed in developing a simple organization which should combine individual freedom with some degree of corporate control and responsibility. His later years were largely devoted to building up such an organization as might be proof against the forces of persecution on the one hand, and on the other against the anarchic and disruptive tendencies of belief in personal revelation and inspiration. This organization has persisted in essentials to the present day.

Towards the end of the seventeenth century, when the days of acute persecution were over, it appeared to many that Quakerism was likely to become the dominant form of Christianity in England. During the eighteenth, in some of the American colonies where religious freedom was greater, its prospects were even brighter. Yet the movement failed to redeem its promise, and in both England and America the Quakers, in proportion to the population, are now a mere handful of people. Why was this? Undoubtedly there were certain grave defects in the presentation of the foundation principle of the Inward Light, which are pertinent to our subject of the nature of the Authority of the Spirit.

The Quakers had entered into a real experience of first-hand acquaintance with God, and they trusted their lives, individual and corporate, to His direct guidance and control in a way that few other Christians had ever dared to do ; but they were hampered in their expression of this living experience by a failure to transcend the dominant thoughts of their time. Such religious philosophy as there was in that century (with the partial exception of the Cambridge Platonists) was rigidly dualistic in its

character.   It separated by a sharp wall of division
the natural from the supernatural, the human from
the Divine.   What the Quakers had really discovered
(or rather re-discovered) was the Divine Immanence,
but they could not express it in the terms familiar
to them and their contemporaries.   The Light in
their souls they felt themselves compelled to regard
as either purely human or else as purely Divine.
Shrinking in horror from the first alternative, which
they assumed would make Christ and His work
unnecessary, they were shut up to the second.   This
virtually carried with it the idea, which has influenced
many Mystics, that the human must be suppressed
in their lives in order that the Divine may have
freedom to operate.   This, as Dr. Rufus Jones has
powerfully shown in his book *The Later Periods of
Quakerism*, was the chief source of the Quietism that
settled down over the Quakers in the eighteenth
century.   Any prompting to religious service which
was not undeniably supernatural must be suppressed
as being " creaturely activity " ; all " the creature "
could rightly do was to wait to be moved, consciously
and undeniably, by the creating and inspiring Spirit.
It is true that their conviction of a Divine Light in
the souls of all men made many of the Quakers ardent
philanthropists, and their chief service to humanity
has been rendered in this field, as in their opposition
to Slavery and War, and their efforts for reform in
the treatment of the criminal and the insane.   But
they have largely failed to influence the religious
thoughts of men.   They never produced a philosopher,
or a poet until the nineteenth century.   Their only
distinguished theologian was Robert Barclay, who
published his *Apology* at the early age of twenty-

eight.   This failure, so the present writer at least is convinced, is the outcome of the dualism that led them to the disparagement of human reason, as if it were necessarily an obstacle to the Spirit's work.   The Quakers were afraid to use their minds in the things of the Spirit ; and they could not move the world with a religion that held cheap the mind of man. Happily they have awakened to their mistake, and the work of religious instruction is now being vigorously prosecuted among them—instruction for the members generally, men and women, and not of a separated class of preachers.

This example is pertinent to our subject as showing the failure of an attempt to make the Spirit into an infallible *outward* authority.   The Quakers, when, like Barclay, they began to argue, virtually tried to put the authority of the Spirit into the place where Catholics set the authority of the Church and Protestants the authority of the Bible.   That this is so may be observed by the reader of Barclay's *Apology*, Prop. III, " On the Scriptures," where he endeavours to show that not the Scripture, but the Spirit, is " the primary *rule* of faith and manners."   Anyone who uses words carefully, as he did, knows that a " rule " is something external, that can be referred to for authoritative information or direction.   The authority of the Spirit is inward authority, and it is an abuse of language to speak of inward authority as a " rule."   Barclay was led into his mistake by the dualism of his thought, which made the Spirit something wholly external to man himself.

" The doctrine of the Inner Light, in its extreme form, is a flat negation of the authority of the

Church, but is itself a religion of authority, and is liable to the same fatal objections as any other theory of absolute authority."[1]

If we are to avoid these errors, we must recover at least the depth and largeness of the thoughts of the Spirit that we find in Paul and " John." They conceive of God present in the Spirit of the risen Jesus, and manifesting Himself, not apart from men, but *in* their renewed personalities. Transformation by the Spirit is not the thrusting into the human soul, by an outside power, of something wholly alien to its true nature. Rather, the new nature *is* the true nature ; it is that for which man was created, when he was " made in the image of God," coming to its own. The " I " that was " crucified with Christ " was a false usurping self ; the true self is the " I " which lives because " Christ liveth in me " (Gal. ii. 20). Christ the Spirit is not only God but is also the immanent life of man—is that for which he was created, the flower and fruit of that Divine Seed within him which has always been his better self, the pledge and the promise that he could become one with God.[2]

[1] Inge, *Authority and the Inner Light* (Liverpool Lecture), p. 19. The present writer believes, however, that Barclay's mistake in calling the Spirit a " rule " was partly due to a fact of his experience —that dependence on the Light of the Spirit had led, in the Quaker body, not to confusion and anarchy, but to a large measure of agreement and unity. There were disruptive tendencies, but they were overcome. This is a consideration of great importance when we think of the true basis of Christian Reunion. The true protection against schism and disorder is not a barbed wire enclosure of creeds and organization, but a real acquaintance with the mind of the Spirit.

[2] Moberly, *Atonement and Personality*, chapter on " The Holy Spirit."

" We need not go up to heaven to bring Christ
down from above, or back to a dim and vanished
age with painful research, to revive a fading image
of the past. He is near us, here and now, the
light of all our seeing, the ever present, inexhaustible
source and well-spring of spiritual life and strength
and joy. In the living experience of every Christian spirit, if we but read it truly, there is the
witness to the abiding presence of another and
higher, raising it ever above itself, the irrefutable
proof that that redeeming, hallowing, saving spirit,
which for a few brief years identified itself with
a perfect human personality, is not a thing of the
past, but a living operating spirit and power,
imparting to every soul that will but open itself to
receive it, the strength, the purity, the peace, of a
life that is one with the very life of God."[1]

[1] John Caird, *Fundamental Ideas of Christianity*, Vol. II, p. 99.

CHAPTER IX

THE OPENING OF THE INWARD EYE

THE principle that the ultimate witness to the truth of God is to be found within and not without the soul of man, that the final Authority in Religion is not outward but inward, lies very deep in the teaching of the New Testament. The author of the first Epistle attributed to John, for example, even in some passages which seem to have a sharp dogmatic ring, finds it there. " Ye have an anointing from the Holy One, and ye all know. I have not written unto you because ye know not the truth, but because ye know it. . . . He that believeth on the Son of God hath the witness in him."[1] Though the writers never attempted, as the early Quakers did, to formulate a doctrine of the Inward Light, it is to this that they, like their Master before them, constantly appeal.

The objection has often been made that to represent all men as having in some measure the Spirit of God, a Divine witness in their own souls, is to render needless the Incarnation and the saving work of Christ for men. The charge has very often been levelled against the Quakers that they cut away the root of Christianity, at any rate if their central

[1] 1 John ii. 20, 21 ; v. 10. In the last passage the Authorised Version had " in himself," which is more emphatic, but the meaning is the same. Even if " him " refers grammatically to the Son of God, the following verse explains that the " witness " is in the " eternal life " which we ourselves have through Him.

principle is carried to its logical conclusion. It seems desirable, therefore, to devote one chapter to the attempt to show a real connection between the principle of Inward Authority, which has been asserted throughout these pages, and the ideas that are commonly regarded as fundamentally Christian.

The connection is to be found in the fact of Sin,[1] and in the effect of Sin in obscuring man's spiritual vision. We need make no assumption, such as since Augustine has been often made, that man is *totally* corrupt, that his power of inward sight is wholly gone. Such an assumption does indeed, in the present writer's judgment at any rate, cut away the foundations of Christianity, and appears to be wholly inconsistent with the teaching of our Lord Himself, who found, in the conduct even of men who were largely " evil," something that provided a real clue to the character of God (Matt. vii. 11). Apart from this gratuitous perversion of its teaching, the New Testament Gospel is based on the reality of man's sinfulness, and on his need of reconciliation with God. This is no theological fiction. Everyone who faces the facts of life, whose eyes are open to the tragedy of human things, must recognise the need. Discord has come into the life of self-conscious beings— discord of a different kind from any that we may think we see in the life of plants and animals, which, speaking broadly, fulfil the law of their being—and man, unaided, is unable to restore the harmony for which his life was intended. Ethical treatises may define the nature of the good, but not one can remedy the divided will, or offer a cure for the general malady, " when I would do good, evil is present with

[1] For the nature of Sin see above, p. 21.

me." Social Utopias have been planned with consummate skill, but have one and all made shipwreck if they have neglected to take account of human selfishness. The great war through which the world has lately passed, and the tragedies that have followed it through a vindictive " peace "—the imminent menace of the total destruction of our civilisation if the war spirit is not transcended in human relations —all this is but a monstrous manifestation of the discord wrought by Sin. A civilisation founded on self-interest, indifferent to the good of the whole, and oblivious of the will of God, destroys itself.

And Sin meets with its inevitable nemesis, not alone in the collective life of humanity, but in the individual life as well. Its effect is to mar and distort, and if persisted in eventually to destroy, the Divine image in the soul of man—that in and for which he was created. It blurs the vision of spiritual realities, hides God and His truth from our view, turns into darkness that which would have been light. It is, says Jesus, the pure in heart who can see God ; of those whose eye is not " single," but is divided between God and mammon, He says, " if therefore the light that is in thee be darkness, how great is the darkness! " (Matt. vi. 22–24). " He that hateth his brother is in the darkness, and walketh in the darkness, and knoweth not whither he goeth, because the darkness hath blinded his eyes " (1 John ii. 11).

" I am come," says the Johannine Christ, " that they which see not may see " (John ix. 39). He makes to man the supreme offer for his supreme need—reconciliation with God, redemption from sin, and with it the opening of the inward eye that sin had well-nigh blinded. It is as we are reconciled to

God, as He takes possession of us, that our spiritual eyes are opened to behold clearly that of which before we were but dimly conscious. But how can we suppose that this offer of reconciliation, and the restoration of sight to the blind, is the prerogative of Christ alone ? Had not prophets and psalmists a true sight of spiritual realities, and, beyond them, the multitudes in all nations who " feared God and worked righteousness," though they had never heard of Jesus ?

It is here that the Johannine thoughts of Christ are specially helpful. He is introduced, in the fourth Gospel, as the Divine Logos who has always been the " life " and " light " of men. After the Prologue, He is not called by that name again, but the thought is there. All men are in some measure " taught of God " (John vi. 45), and some of them " hear " and " learn " from Him. In the fulness of time " the Logos becomes flesh " ; the diffused light is (as was said above) focussed in a perfect human personality, in whom therefore the Father is revealed. Those who have been truly " hearing and learning " from the Father come gladly to this clearer Light as soon as it is made known to them ; while those who do evil turn their backs upon it (iii. 20, 21). It is quite clear that the author feels no contradiction between the statements " They shall all be taught of God " and " No man cometh unto the Father but by me " (xiv. 6). It *was* through the eternal Logos that they had been taught of God even before they knew Christ in the flesh ; those who were " of the truth " and took heed to the teaching embraced with joy the fuller revelation as soon as it came to them. The thought is not that these can do without the " new

H

birth " of the Spirit ; it is that they are in such an
attitude of soul that they receive with open arms the
fuller life, and come gladly to the Father whom Christ
reveals but whom before they had known but dimly.

The essential work of Jesus, as presented in this
Gospel, is to communicate *life* to men—to bring them
out of the death and darkness of sin into the life and
light of God.   This life and light is offered to all who
will come into a right relation to Himself—a relation
variously   described   as   " believing,"   " receiving,"
" knowing," " hearing," " seeing " Him.   The relation to God into which this brings them is identical
with that which Paul calls Reconciliation and Adop-
tion.   It is the sharing in the sonship of Christ.
And those who thus come to share the sonship of
Christ share also, according to their measure, His
clearness of spiritual vision.

These are not mere words of conventional piety.
They stand for an experience, to the reality of which
many can testify.   There is a real difference between
the vague, germ-like faculty of inward vision possessed by mankind in general, and the power that
comes with the reception into our souls, not as a
creed but as a heart-cleansing experience, of the clear
light that shines in the face of Jesus Christ.   It is,
indeed, the pure in heart who see ; it is those whose
inward nature is renewed by the Spirit of the Crucified
who come into full possession of their powers of
spiritual vision.   He has, it is true, never been far
from any of us.   Without our knowing it, He

" Is yet the fountain light of all our day,
    Is yet the master light of all our seeing ; "

but life is a new thing to us when we discern that

this light, which has been but as a vaguely-conceived principle, is no other than the Light of the World which shines in the person of our Lord.

That which before was but a dim foreshadowing, a far-off ideal—a better nature which we vainly strove, or else cared not, to make our own—has taken visible form, once for all, before our eyes. The life and sacrificial death of Jesus present to us at once the reality of our own true nature, and the very heart of God Himself. He wins us by sharing our humanity, even unto death, that we may share His life and light. The promise of His Spirit is the promise that the work is to be effectual, if we will have it so—that He, our better self, shall become our actual self, that we shall begin to see with His eyes. This clearing of our spiritual vision, this enlightening and expansion of the normal faculties of the soul, is the correlative of the Inward Authority with which the Truth of God appeals to us, and the condition of knowing its power.

CHAPTER X

WHAT, then, is the net upshot, and what are the practical bearings, of our discussion of the nature and function of Authority in Religion ? The questions that have been before us are alive and pressing. We have been endeavouring to find a safe anchorage, " within the veil " that hides the things of the spirit from our mortal gaze, for souls that are storm-tossed and drifting, unable to accept the outward authorities that are offered them, but not yet strong enough to trust the Authority within. The number of these drifting souls is increasing fast. That many of them are earnest seekers after truth is evidenced by the wide demand for every live book on religion. The light of scientific criticism is upon the creeds and standards of the past, and they are shrivelling before our eyes. Even in the Roman Church there is revolt against despotic authority, and a reaching forth after a more inward and spiritual support. In all the Protestant churches the number is continually growing of those who know that the Bible is not infallible ; but the teachers are few who follow up effectually the lead of the first Reformers, and fearlessly point the seekers to the Light of the Spirit in their hearts.

It has been a part of the writer's purpose to show that each of the outward authorities that men have set up to control their beliefs and conduct has its fitting place, but that not one of them is final or absolute. There needs must be Authority, for each one of us is born into this world not as an isolated unit whose whole experience is to be gained *de novo*, but as a member of society which is what it is through the long heritage of the past. Into the thoughts and ways and conventions of the community we all grow up, and it is at our own risk that we try to thrust them aside. In giving them a large place for the direction of our lives we do not weaken our own personality, we help it to develop normally. But as soon as ever the community begins to assert its sway as final and absolute, it crushes the growth of the individual and partially destroys the very material out of which alone a healthy society can be built. Such a community becomes stagnant and decadent. Only as collective authority gives place to personal autonomy, only as it trains the individual to perceive and follow for himself the true and the good, only as it leaves him increasingly free to obey the inward authority that speaks in the depth of his own soul, will it be strong and progressive.

The authority of the Church will be ever round about those who are seeking for light and truth, as a spiritual home where, in the warmth of Christian fellowship, they may learn to share the treasures that have been garnered by the spiritual struggles of the past. That authority is in essence the unity of the Christian consciousness—the collective experience and testimony of all saintly souls who have learned through Jesus Christ that God is their Father, and have lived and wrought in a common sense of sonship with Him, in a common dependence on His Spirit. Any new thought that comes to an individual Christian he will always desire to test and temper, by comparing it with what has been revealed to others richer, stronger and more devoted than himself, whether in the past or the present. He will not presumptuously claim it as the direct word of God to himself without this preliminary testing, remembering always that he has the treasure in an earthen vessel, that he is not infallible. Yet, since this personal touch with God is the very root and centre of the Christian life, without which the collective authority of the Church would have no existence, that which he believes to have been revealed to him must, when it has been duly pondered and tested, take precedence over all outward authority. Had the prophets of humanity thought otherwise, they would have " quenched the Spirit," and failed to lead the world forward to a fuller knowledge of the truth.

It may be that with many of us the chief difficulty is the absence of any such convincing and compelling sense of Divine communion and communication. The apparent " silence of God " weighs down our spirit. Then it is, especially, that we may be helped to rise into a larger and stronger faith by considering the experience of those who have gone before us. In the beautiful words of the Dean of St. Paul's :

" But for the testimony of the great cloud of witnesses, who have mounted higher and seen more, I should not have ventured to build so much on this immediate revelation of God to the human soul. But the evidence of the saints seems to me absolutely trustworthy ; and the dimness of my own vision would be disquieting only if I

felt that I had deserved better. The pearl of
great price is not so easily found. But do we
know of any who have sought after the knowledge
of God as diligently as other men seek after wealth
and honour, and have come away [finally] empty-
handed ? "[1]

That is the foundation of Church authority, and it
is for each of us to add to its volume.

The Authority of the Bible, granted a measure of
this personal knowledge of God, will be to us no theory
reached by painful and sophistical argument, but a
living reality, felt and accepted, because we have
come for ourselves into an experience akin to that of
prophets, psalmists and apostles, and understand by
spiritual sympathy something of the truths they
struggled to express. While Criticism takes from
us much that we with others may have held dear,
it leaves the student, if he is at once open-hearted and
humble and receptive, with the assurance that God has
not left His sad world to grope after Him as best it
may. The conviction that He has progressively
revealed His mind and will to those who have diligently sought Him, and that this great process of
progressive revelation, culminating in Jesus Christ,
is recorded in the pages of Scripture as nowhere else
in the world's literature, is placed on a far stronger
basis when once it has been thoroughly tested and not
found wanting. What genuine Criticism does is not
to impose upon the Bible any ready-made notions
of our own, such as, on the one hand, that being
" inspired " it contains no mistakes, or, on the
other, that any event which appears miraculous must

[1] Inge, *Outspoken Essays* (Second Series), p. 15.

be ruled out as unreal. The true Christian student humbly submits his mind to the facts, to learn how God has actually revealed Himself to men ; he does not presumptuously refuse to accept a revelation unless he can first be assured that it is the pure truth of God without any admixture of human imperfection and error. He learns that it was only by slow degrees that men's eyes were opened, and that consequently the teaching of one age differs vastly from that of another. To gain some knowledge of the process of revelation, he has to study the relative dates of the books of the Bible and of their component parts, in order that he may not unwittingly attribute to one age ideas that really belong to another. It is true that he always needs " the testimony of the Spirit," the witness of a growing religious experience in his own soul, if he is to interpret truly what he reads. But this " testimony " must be understood to cover all the light that unbiased study can bring to a mind that is humble and sympathetic and receptive.[1]

The authority of Jesus Christ will always be for the Christian the greatest of the outward authorities that must help to mould his beliefs and regulate his conduct. It is still to Him that the Scriptures testify, even when they are read in the full light of criticism.

[1] It may seem to some that this places the interpretation of Scripture out of the reach of the unlearned. The answer is that the difficulty will lessen as the Bible becomes better known, and that a right understanding of theological doctrines is not necessary for beginning or maintaining the Christian life, however essential it may be for taking a useful part in controversy. The *translation* of the Bible is a matter for which we have to trust the experts, but their general agreement makes it available for the unlearned also. There seems no reason why, in time, the same should not be true of its *interpretation*.

He remains for us the centre of our faith, the ground
of our assurance that we really know something of
the character and mind of God. He satisfies our
deepest longings as philosophy can never do, by
giving us, at the back of all our problems, not merely
a Universal Consciousness, but a heart of Universal
Love. We recognise His authority as that of the
eternal Word of God. We bow before it with un-
measured reverence, because it is He who has reconciled us to God and brought us into the communion
with God in which Authority regains its meaning.
Yet, when we ask how His authority is available for
men, we are driven to answer, not through any
infallible record of His spoken words when here on
earth, nor through any mechanical attempt to copy
His deeds ; but through the presence of His living
Spirit in our hearts. Welcoming all the light which
the most careful study can throw upon His person,
His works and His words, we shall shun as irreverence
and " pride of heart " the attempt to impose upon
history an interpretation due either to the human
dogmas that have come down to us from the past,
or to negations begotten by a too-limited philosophy
of our own. We shall be, at all costs, loyal to the
facts we find. Yet this humility and loyalty to truth,
though it may lead us to deny some things, and to
suspend judgment on others, that have been taught
us concerning His life on earth, will not mar or blur
the clearness of our direct intuition of His character
and His personality. Thanks largely to critical
study, that intuition may be brighter for us to-day
than in any Christian century since the first. Criticism has helped to remove the " deadly familiarity "
of the Gospel pages, to take off the wrappings that

have concealed the person of our Lord. Thanks to
its aid, many are finding in some of the simplest
Gospel stories, so simple as to be intelligible to the
youngest child, depths beyond depths of spiritual
meaning, and the profoundest knowledge of the
human soul and its hidden needs. We are constrained
to acknowledge that " Never man so spake." One
who knows as Jesus knew, who sees with this depth
of spiritual insight, must, we feel, be worthy of our
trust. And so to Him belongs without measure that
authority which we concede, in some degree, to all
who can see further, and who know more, than others.

And yet this is no blind trust. We need, finally,
the Authority of the Spirit in our own souls if we are
truly to understand Him, or the Scriptures that
testify of Him. It was upon this inward authority,
not the outward authority of the record of His words
and deeds, that His first followers rested. We do
not really honour Him if, in would-be but mistaken
reverence, we close the eyes of our own reason and
judgment, and adopt the " credo quia impossibile."
He is really our Lord as in freedom and boldness we
use the Light that is given us, enter into the place of
experience and insight where we can discern truth
for ourselves, and know that things are not true
because Jesus said them, but that He said them because
they are true. Deep below all outward authority
is the inward authority of the Spirit, as that which
alone makes truth living and not dead, and gives
it vital power over our lives. The better we know,
by this inward Light, the character of our Master,
the more fully shall we understand what it was
that inspired His first followers, and be ready to

believe in, and to trust for ourselves, the present inspiration of His Spirit.

Chief among the causes that appear to prevent Christians from trusting more fully, like the first disciples, to the living Spirit of their Master, is the fear that they will not keep together—that they will fancy themselves led in divergent paths of belief or conduct, and that there will be no common standard by which to judge. Is not this in reality a lack of faith in God ? The Spirit is *one*, as Paul affirms again and again in 1 Cor. xii, and so is the life of the Spirit in the members of the body of Christ—though that life may manifest itself in many different ways. If the members follow the Spirit faithfully, in love to one another as he says in the next chapter, they will hold together in unity. That was the Apostle's faith, and it was largely justified in the issue, imperfect as the churches were. So far as they followed the Spirit's guidance, and sought to live in love, they were preserved in fellowship and in a large measure of agreement. Parties indeed appeared at Corinth, and even Apostles quarrelled at times with one another ; but none of these imperfections wrecked the infant Church. While no one was infallible, their human limitations never upset their serene confidence in the inward Guide and Teacher whom their Master had promised, and who was a felt reality in their lives.

As this consciousness of the Spirit declined, it seemed that the only way to preserve unity was to define " the faith," and to set up a rigid organization. The Church " played for safety," unwilling to make the venture of the path of faith. The unity so attained was but superficial and apparent. Vast numbers were cut off from the Church—Arians, Nestorians, Monophysites and the rest—many of whom were just as truly Christian as those who accepted the formulæ and the discipline. The Church had not the courage to trust what Mr. Clutton-Brock called the "scent for truth" that would eventually have kept these, or brought them, into a right relation to Jesus Christ. The real remedy for "heresy" is a vigorous spiritual life, and a trust in the healthy instinct which knows what doctrine ministers to life and what does not, which will adopt the one and refuse the other.

If we look for an illustration on a smaller scale, we may find it in the Society of Friends. That body has tried to rest its whole Church polity on experience of Divine guidance, individual and collective, and, while maintaining this trust in the authority of the Spirit, it has kept together. Amidst much divergence of thought there has been, in this country, no important division, and it is probably a more united body than most of those that have trusted to outward authorities of creed and organization.

The real unity of Christians is not in these outward things, but in their common experience of the one Lord, and the one Spirit, whose life, like the sap in the living vine, flows through them all. It is not by agreement on formal creeds or ritual observances that we can know the fulfilment of the prayer "that they all may be one." Opinions and practices divide, but facts and truth unite. Already, in all churches, men and women are being drawn together in the fellowship of those who "walk in the light," who are "of the truth," who have forsaken the religions of dogma for the religion of the Spirit. Below all our

surface differences there is the substantial unity
of those who worship the same Lord, whose minds
are open to the same facts, who have been lifted by
Him into the same Christian experience, which is
fellowship with the Father and with His Son Jesus
Christ.   So far as they walk in His light, they have
fellowship one with another, and their spiritual eyes
are opened through an inward experience of His
" blood," which " keeps on cleansing them from sin."

   " As for you, the anointing which ye received of
him abideth in you, and ye need not that any one
teach you ; but as his anointing teacheth you concerning all things, and is true, and is no lie, even as it
taught you, abide in him."   (1 John ii. 27.)

INDEX